the ULTIMATE BOOK OF preteen DEVOTIONS

Group
Loveland, Colorado

Group's R.E.A.L. Guarantee® to you:

This Group resource incorporates our R.E.A.L. approach to ministry—one that encourages long-term retention and life transformation. It's ministry that's:

Relational
Because learner-to-learner interaction enhances learning and builds Christian friendships.

Experiential
Because what learners experience through discussion and action sticks with them up to 9 times longer than what they simply hear or read.

Applicable
Because the aim of Christian education is to equip learners to be both hearers and doers of God's Word.

Learner-based
Because learners understand and retain more when the learning process takes into consideration how they learn best.

The Ultimate Book of Preteen Devotions

Visit our Web site: **www.grouppublishing.com**

Credits
Contributing Authors: Teryl Cartwright, Jan Kershner, Julie Meiklejohn, Christina Schofield, Bonnie Temple, and Vicki L.O. Witte
Editors: Vicki L.O. Witte and Jim Hawley
Chief Creative Officer: Joani Schultz
Copy Editor: Ann M. Diaz
Art Director: Kari K. Monson
Illustrator: Jan Knudson
Cover Art Director/Designer: Bambi Eitel
Production Manager: Peggy Naylor

Library of Congress Cataloging-in-Publication Data
The ultimate book of preteen devotions.
    p. cm.
    Includes indexes.
    ISBN 0-7644-2588-9 (pbk. : alk. paper)
    1. Christian education of preteens. 2. Christian education--Activity programs.
3. Bible--Study and teaching. I. Group Publishing.
    BV1475.9.U45 2003
    268'.432--dc21   2003005970

10 9 8 7 6 5 4 3 2 1   12 11 10 09 08 07 06 05 04 03
Printed in the United States of America.

Table of Contents

Introduction

Are your preteens tired of boring, go-nowhere, do-nothing devotions? Are you looking for Scripture-based devotions that really touch your kids where they live? If so, then *The Ultimate Book of Preteen Devotions* is for you!

God's truth has the potential to touch preteens (and adults!) in a wide variety of ways. Some people respond best to words, while others respond best to pictures, and still others need to move around or create something in order to learn best. Some people respond to music, others to stories or videos, and still others to science experiments. God's truth can work through all of these avenues!

In the following pages, you'll find dozens of active, inviting experiences that take Scriptural truths and bring them to life for your kids. Your preteens will gain a deeper understanding of what God's Word means in their lives through a variety of sensory and experiential activities. You'll find devotions to help preteens explore what's important to them: their faith, their friendships, their family relationships, school, their world, and special days.

The Ultimate Book of Preteen Devotions is an essential tool for any leader interested in shaping preteens' lives with biblical truths. It's designed to be used in a variety of settings, from camps, retreats, and overnighters, to Sunday school, midweek meetings, Bible study groups, and club settings. Use *The Ultimate Book of Preteen Devotions* any time preteens are gathered together and have Bibles they've brought or you've provided. And get ready for unique, life-changing devotions that will inspire your preteens to live what they believe!

Section 1:
Devotions About Faith

God's Word Power

Theme: The Bible

Scripture: Hebrews 4:12

Summary: Kids will experiment with seltzer water and compare it to the power of God's Word.

Preparation: You'll need a bottle of seltzer (or tonic) water and a few raisins for each pair of students, as well as several towels. Please use an uncarpeted area for this devotion or go outdoors.

Begin by saying: **Listen to a description of the power of God's Word.** Read aloud Hebrews 4:12, slowly and with expression. Then ask:

• **How was this description of God's Word surprising or different than you expected?**

Say: **Let's do an experiment to remind us that God's Word is active.**

Have students find partners. Give each pair of students an unopened bottle of seltzer water and a few raisins. Tell students to remove the labels from their bottles so they can see inside. Then have them open the bottles and drop the raisins inside. Have them share what happens to the raisins. Then say: **Just as the raisins were set into motion by the water, God's Word is active inside of us. The Bible helps us grow and change and do unexpected things, just as the water unexpectedly caused the raisins to move around in the bottles.** Ask:

• **What are some ways you think God's Word is living and active in your life?**

Say: **God's Word is not only active, but strong. Our verse says that God's**

Word is more powerful than a sword. Let's try another experiment to picture how God's Word can be so strong.

Hold up a bottle of seltzer water and its lid. Ask:

• **Which is stronger, the bottle cap or the water inside?**

Have students put the lids back on their bottles. Ask them to stand in a line, with partners standing beside each other. They should take turns vigorously shaking their bottles with the lids pointed away from their faces. Let them use the towels to clean up the water that escapes from the bottles. Then ask:

• **How did the water become more powerful than the lid of the container?**

• **How does what happened to the water remind you of the power of God's Word? How will that change how you read God's Word this week?**

Say: **God's Word, the Bible, is powerful because it comes from God. It's more powerful than we are. We can't keep it bottled up or pretend that it isn't active in our lives. Just like this water, God's powerful Word does unexpected things and can't be contained. God's Word is the ultimate word for us, because just like water, we need it in order to live.**

This messy activity may work best outdoors! We also recommend that kids twist the bottle lids on only halfway so there is less danger of the lids popping off. Don't allow kids to point their bottles at each other.

Heavenly Havens

Theme: Heaven

Scripture: John 14:1-6

Summary: Preteens will make houses from cards and then blueprints of those houses. Then they'll discuss the home Jesus has prepared for them in heaven.

Preparation: You'll need lots of index cards—about fifty for each pair of students. You'll also need clear tape and pencils for everyone. Have graph paper on hand if available; otherwise, use plain paper.

When students arrive, have them choose partners. Distribute cards, tape, paper, and pencils. Ask each pair to create a deluxe house of cards. They can tape the cards to make their houses a little sturdier. When they've finished, ask them to use the paper and pencils to draw blueprints of their houses, labeling each room.

Instead of index cards, feel free to use cards from family games or card decks for this activity. However, be advised that they might get bent or wrecked by tape, so don't plan to use the cards again! You might raid local thrift stores and garage sales to stock up on cards.

Next, provide a little time for "home tours," giving preteens the opportunity to show off their mansions to their classmates. When they've finished, spend a little time talking about their own houses and how their bedrooms are decorated. Ask:

• **What is your favorite thing about your bedroom?**

• **What would you like to add or change about your room?**

Ask students to read John 14:1-6 silently, and then discuss the verses aloud. Get students thinking about their house in heaven. Ask for their ideas about what their future room might look like!

Say: **Think about what it's like when you're at camp or on vacation. You may have a good time and see a lot, but you never get too comfortable because you know you aren't staying long. You aren't home. That's the attitude we should have about our time here on earth. We don't ever get too comfortable here because our real home is with God.** Ask:

• **What special care has God put into our home in heaven?**

• **How will life in heaven be different from life on earth?**

• **Have you secured a reservation for a heaven? Why or why not?**

To close, distribute paper and pencils and allow students to discuss and draw up a house plan for their dream home in heaven.

Power!

Theme: The Holy Spirit

Scripture: Acts 1:8; Galatians 5:22-23

Summary: Kids will build a simple hovercraft and compare its power to the Holy Spirit in their lives.

Preparation: Before class, cut the necks from two-liter plastic soda bottles, leaving about a one-inch skirt on each one. Cut an X (about one-inch lines) in the center of the bottom of plastic foam bowls. You'll need a bottleneck and a bowl for each preteen. Assemble one hovercraft before class by pushing the spout and neck of a plastic bottle through the X in a bowl so that it pokes out the bottom of the bowl. (See illustration.) When you invert the bowl and set the hovercraft on a hard surface, the bowl should rest squarely on the surface. If it doesn't, trim some plastic off the bottleneck. You'll also need pens or markers.

Be careful not to cut too large an X in the bowls. If the hole gets too big, you can seal around the spout with tape.

Ask a volunteer to read aloud Galatians 5:22-23. Then say: **As Christians, our goal is to become more and more like Jesus.** Ask:

• **What are some ways we should be like Jesus? What are some of his characteristics or attitudes that we should imitate?**

If you don't have enough two-liter bottles for each student to have one, divide kids into small groups, and have them work together on the hovercrafts.

As kids mention Christlike ways, if appropriate, translate them into fruits of the Spirit. For example, if they say, "We shouldn't say bad things about friends behind their backs," you could write on the board: "no gossip," then, "kindness" or "goodness."

Say: **Oftentimes we don't measure up to the list in Galatians 5, but God wants to help us.** Let's make something fun to illustrate how God helps us. Pass out the hovercraft supplies, and show kids how to put the pieces together, but don't tell them what it is they're making.

When everyone is finished, have kids choose a few of the fruits of the Spirit that they think they need most in their lives and write the words on their hovercraft. Write some words on your own hovercraft, too. When the kids are finished, collect the markers, and set your hovercraft on a smooth surface, such as a tabletop or uncarpeted floor.

Say: **Let's say this bowl represents my life. I'm supposed to be like Christ, but sometimes it's hard. I can move this bowl around, but it's not powered by anything, so I have to push it with my hand, throw it, spin the top, or do something like that. That's like me trying to be a Christian on my own strength, trying to be good, kind, joyful, and so on. It just doesn't work sometimes. I'll show you a simple way to power this bowl.** Blow into the spout so the hovercraft moves around the table. You don't need to put your mouth on the spout—just blow into it.

When I blow into this spout, it fills the bowl with air, creating an air cushion and moving the bowl. It's called a hovercraft. Real hovercrafts use fans

to drive air under them, creating a cushion of air. By controlling the direction of the air, you can make a hovercraft go where you want it to go. Experiment with your hovercraft for a few minutes, then we'll talk about it.

Encourage kids to try making the hovercrafts go where they want them to go. The hovercrafts often scoot backward, but encourage kids to keep experimenting. Then have them try to blow the hovercrafts to each other. After several minutes, have everyone stop.

Ask a volunteer to read aloud Acts 1:8. Then ask:

• **What did Jesus say his disciples would receive when the Holy Spirit came on them?**

Say: **Jesus promised them "power"! That meant power to do everything he wanted them to do. It's the same thing for you and me. God wants to fill you with his Holy Spirit and empower you, just as air powered our hovercrafts today.** Ask:

• **What was easy or hard about moving your hovercraft?**

• **How is that like or unlike the Holy Spirit in your life?**

Say: **It may have been hard to control the hovercraft's direction or speed, but it was easy to get it to move by blowing in it. Let's remember to ask the Holy Spirit to fill us and help us be like Jesus this week!**

A Cog in the Machine

Theme: The Church

Scripture: 1 Corinthians 12:12-26

Summary: Groups of students will make "machines" using their bodies and then talk about their roles as members of the church, the body of Christ.

Preparation: You'll need various simple props, such as a chair, some beanbags, and some large pots and pans (optional).

Have students form groups of four to six people. Say: **Time to put on your inventor caps! Today you're going to create working "machines." The tools and materials you will use consist only of the people in your groups and these props.** Indicate the props chosen.

You can create any kind of machine—something similar to an existing machine or a completely imaginary machine. There are a few rules. First, each person in your group has to be an important part of the machine. Second, each part of the machine has to have a specific task to do. For example, if you create a wicket mover, one person might pick up the wicket and pass it over

his or her head to the next machine "part." That person might take the wicket and spin around with it and then toss it to the next "part." The next person might give the wicket a "spit shine" before kicking it to the next person, and so on. Be creative with your machines, and have fun!

Circulate while groups are creating their machines to provide guidance and answer questions. Give groups about ten minutes to create their machines, and then have each group demonstrate and explain its machine to the whole class. Encourage groups to give each other big rounds of applause, and then have kids sit down. Ask:

• **Were all of the parts of your machine equally important? Why or why not?**

• **What would have happened if you had removed one of the parts? Would your machine still work as well?**

Ask a volunteer from each group to read aloud a portion of 1 Corinthians 12:12-26. Then ask:

• **What does this passage tell you about the parts of your body?**

• **How is that like your machines?**

• **How is that like people in the church?**

Say: **This passage uses the body as a way to talk about people's "jobs" as Christians. Just as the body needs all of its parts to function properly, the church needs all of its people and their gifts and talents in order to function well and bring the light of Christ into the world.** Ask:

• **What do you think your job in the church might be? What are some special gifts and talents you bring?**

Say: **This week, spend some time thinking about the special, important job you have as a Christian. Think about the God-given gifts and talents you have to offer, and think about ways you can use those gifts and talents to help more people hear and know about the good news of Christ.**

Loving, Caring

Theme: Loving Jesus

Scripture: John 21:15-22

Summary: Students will interact with pets and spend time caring for them. Then they'll talk about how caring for others shows our love for Jesus.

Preparation: You'll need some small pets, plus food for the animals, grooming supplies, and supplies to clean out their cages, aquariums, litter pans, and so on.

Before class, arrange for friends within your church to share their small pets with your class. Small indoor animals such as kittens, hamsters, fish, gerbils, and birds will work best.

When students arrive, allow them to interact with the animals. Then ask preteens to take care of the animals, brushing their fur, cleaning out their cages or aquariums, and filling their food and water dishes. After a few minutes, ask:

- **How do most people feel about their pets?**
- **What sort of person neglects or mistreats a pet?**

Ask students to read John 21:15-22. Then say: **Jesus makes it clear that the way to show we love him is to care for those around us. Obviously, caring for people is a little different than caring for pets.** Ask:

- **What did Jesus mean when he told Peter to "feed my sheep"?**
- **What are some needs of people that you know?**
- **What are you doing to meet those needs?**
- **How does caring for others show Jesus what he means to us?**

To close, spend time brainstorming ways to love Jesus by meeting specific needs. Pray for those needs, and make a plan to meet them.

Pressure Papers

Theme: Obedience

Scripture: Acts 5:29b

Summary: Kids will cover themselves with "pressures" they face every day. Then they'll discuss how staying focused on obeying God, rather than people, will help them make good choices.

Preparation: You'll need a supply of large sticky notes and fine-tipped markers.

Say: **Think of some of the pressures you feel every day. Write as many pressures as you can think of on these sticky notes, one pressure per paper.**

Encourage kids to come up with as many pressures as they can in two minutes. Some examples of positive pressures might include: "Get an A on my book report," "Score a goal in soccer," or "Play my violin solo without messing up." Examples of negative pressures might include: "Joining in gossip," "Swearing," or "Watching movies my parents have forbidden."

Call time, and say: **Wow! Look at all those pressures!** Ask:

• **Were you surprised at how many pressures you came up with in such a short time? Explain.**

Ask for a few volunteers to share some of their pressures. Then ask:

• **What do you think of the pressures you just heard? Are they good, bad, or neither? Explain.**

Say: **Some of the pressures you mentioned were good, like trying to get good grades. And some were bad, like peer pressure to do things you know are wrong. Let's see what it's like to go through a typical day trying to face these pressures.**

Have kids stand in a circle holding their "pressure papers." Go around the circle, having each preteen read aloud one pressure and then placing the sticky note somewhere on his or her clothing or body. Keep going around the circle until kids are wearing all their sticky notes.

Say: **It looks as though you have lots of pressure and choices to make every day! There are all these expectations to live up to and all these temptations to face.** Ask:

• **How does it feel to face all these pressures every day? Explain.**

• **How do you decide what or whom to obey?**

Invite a student to read aloud Acts 5:29b while the others read along in their Bibles.

Say: **Keeping our eyes on God will help us stay on the right path. If we keep this verse in mind, it'll be easier to ignore the negative pressures we face. But what about the positive pressures?**

Sometimes we get so caught up trying to please everyone else that we forget God in our daily lives. For example, it's more important to obey God's rule of being kind than it is to make the cheerleading squad. See what I mean?

Let's get rid of these pressures and stay focused on obeying God!

Go around the circle again. Have each person repeat Acts 5:29b aloud and then remove all of the sticky notes and throw them in the trash. Finally, lead kids in a prayer asking God to help them obey his ways, not the ways of the world.

Swept Away

Theme: Forgiveness

Scripture: Isaiah 44:22

Summary: Kids will play a game in which they sweep away "paper sins." Then they'll learn from the Bible that God can sweep their sins away completely.

Preparation: Tear sheets of paper in half. You'll need several half-sheets for each student. You'll also need pencils and a broom.

Have kids form pairs, and give each pair a pencil and a supply of scrap paper. Ask partners to think of sins that people their age often face. For example, kids might think of such sins as cheating, disobeying parents, or gossiping. Tell partners to condense the sins they think of into one-word descriptions and to write a one-word sin on each piece of paper.

After a few minutes, go around the room and let each pair read the sins they wrote to the rest of the class. (If one partner wrote on the papers, the other partner could read the sins aloud.)

Say: **That's a lot of sins! But that's not surprising, since we *all* sin.**

Have partners discuss the following questions. After each one, invite volunteers to share their answers with the rest of the class. Ask:

• **How do you feel after you sin?**

• **Is there any way to undo the sins you commit? Explain.**

Say: **Once we've sinned, there's nothing we can do to undo that sin. It's just not humanly possible. But God can do it! In a few minutes, we'll read a Bible verse that explains what I mean. But first, let's play a game as an introduction.**

Have partners divide their papers evenly, each taking half. Preteens should stand in a circle, with one student standing in the center with a broom. Have kids crumple their papers into wads. They should roll their paper wads across the circle as the student in the center sweeps them out of the circle with the broom. Let the kids in the circle retrieve the paper wads as they're swept out and roll them back inside the circle. After a minute or so, choose a new sweeper and play again. Play several times, letting new students do the sweeping. Then have kids sit in a circle.

Say: **This game gave us a silly introduction to an important Bible truth. In this game, the person with the broom was able to sweep away almost all of the sin papers, right? In reality, God can sweep away all of our sins. Listen to what the Bible says.** Have a volunteer read aloud Isaiah 44:22 while the other students follow along in their Bibles. Then ask:

• **When does God sweep away our sins?**

• **Why do you think God is willing to sweep away our sins and forgive us so completely?**

• **How does knowing about God's incredible forgiveness make you feel about him? act toward him?**

Have kids return to their pairs. Close by letting partners pray for each other, asking for God's forgiveness and for the strength to repent.

Re-paint-ance

Theme: Repentance

Scripture: Psalm 51:1-12

Summary: Students will paint over an already-painted canvas and then talk about the changes that repentance brings.

Preparation: You'll need a few old paintings. Check with local thrift stores or a high school art department to see if they have any available. Students will need acrylic paints, brushes, and containers of water. Newspapers can be used to protect tabletops, and plastic trash bags make practical paint shirts when holes are cut for head and arms. The paint is permanent—so plan accordingly!

As students arrive, assign them to small groups. Each group will receive a painted canvas. The number of students per group will be determined by how many paintings you have. Distribute paint and brushes, and ask students to work together to paint a new picture right over the top of the existing one.

When they have finished their masterpieces, allow them to share their work with their classmates.

Explain that what they have just done is called *pentimento* in art circles. This is an Italian term that means *repentance*. It describes the practice of painting over a pre-existing painting, showing that an artist has changed his mind about the first painting. Ask:

- **Why might an artist change his or her mind about a painting?**

Ask volunteers to read aloud Psalm 51:1-12, and then discuss the idea of repentance. Help students understand the context of this passage—David approached God for forgiveness, repenting of his sins of adultery and murder.

Say: **Repentance is more than just feeling sorry about something bad we've done. True repentance brings about a change in our behavior. We decide we don't like the picture sin has painted in our lives, and we start fresh. With God's help, we make something completely new and better out of our lives.** Ask:

- **Why isn't it enough to just feel bad about our sins?**
- **How does it feel to get a fresh start after you've messed something up really badly?**
- **Is the new picture you are painting with your actions and attitudes**

better or worse than the old life you are painting over?

• **Are there sins you need to confess and turn from now?**

Students should feel no pressure to answer the last question aloud. Instead, invite them to spend some time contemplating it silently in prayer.

Practice Makes Perfect

Theme: Faith

Scripture: James 2:17

Summary: Preteens will attempt three tasks that usually take considerable practice to do successfully. Then they'll compare their experience to having faith without actions.

Preparation: Set up three centers in your room. At the first center, set out five plastic golf balls. At the second, set out a musical instrument and a complicated piece of sheet music for that instrument. At the third center, provide a mathematical equation for kids to solve. Make sure the equation is far above your kids' skill level. You'll also need a sheet of newsprint and a marker or a chalkboard and chalk.

Gather students together. Ask kids to call out the names of their favorite sports stars. Write the names on a sheet of newsprint. Then point to each name in turn and ask:

• **How did this person get so good?**

Say: **Hmm. That's very interesting. Practice seems to be pretty important in getting good at a sport.** Ask:

• **What other kinds of activities require plenty of practice?**

• **When has practice helped you personally?**

Say: **Practice not only helps us excel in sports, it also helps us in lots of other areas. You learned multiplication by practicing your times tables, right? And you learned to read by practicing. If you play an instrument, you know that you had to practice scales before you could play a song. Practice is important!**

Now let's see what happens when practice isn't a part of the equation.

Have kids form three groups, and have each group go to one of the stations you prepared. Tell the kids in one group to take turns showing off their juggling skills with the five plastic golf balls. Tell kids in the next group to take turns playing the sheet music you provided. Tell kids in the third group to take turns solving the mathematical equation. After several minutes, call time. Ask:

• **Well, how did you do? Were you good at these tasks? Why or why not?**

• **How could you have been more skilled at these tasks?**

Say: **It's hard to do something well if you don't practice. It's the same way with our faith. Without exercise—practice—our faith isn't going to win any awards. Here's what I mean.**

Have a student read aloud James 2:17 as others follow along. Then ask:

• **What do you think this verse means?**

• **What's an example of faith that's not accompanied by action?** If kids seem stumped, encourage them to read verses 14-16.

• **What's an example of faith** *with* **action? an example in your life?**

Close by having kids commit to exercise their faith in the coming week. Ask students to think of at least one specific way they can show their faith, and then at your next meeting ask kids to report back on their progress.

Resistance Is Not Futile

Theme: Temptation

Scripture: 1 Corinthians 10:12-13

Summary: Kids will play Sharks 'n' Minnows and then compare the game with facing temptations.

Preparation: You'll need a large open area, such as a gym or outdoors.

Begin by having preteens line up across one end of the open space. Choose one volunteer to be the Shark. That person should stand in the middle of the field or gym. Explain that the Shark will call out, "I dare you to try to get past me," or some other words tempting kids to cross over. Then the Minnows (all the other players) must try to run to the other side of the field without being tagged. Anyone that the Shark tags must join him or her in the middle, tempting others to cross and trying to tag them. Continue play until only one Minnow is left untagged—the winner.

After the game, call preteens together. Discuss these questions:

• **How did it feel when you made it across the field without getting tagged? Why?**

• **How was the Shark in this game like temptations that call you?**

• **How was trying to cross the field without getting tagged like trying to resist temptations without falling into them?**

• **How did it feel to get caught and then go after others? Why?**

• **Toward the end of the game, did you want to get caught by the Sharks? Why or why not?**

• **What makes temptations so tempting?**

Read aloud 1 Corinthians 10:12-13. Say: **The Bible tells us to be careful that we don't fall into temptation when we think we're standing firm.** Ask:

• **How is that like the game we played?**

• **How is that like real life?**

Say: **The Bible also tells us that God won't let us be tempted beyond what we can bear, and that he will always provide a way out.** Ask:

• **In the game, what did you have to do to resist the Sharks? What made it more difficult?**

• **In real life, what makes temptations hard to resist?**

• **How does God help?**

• **How can you resist temptations this week?**

Close by inviting preteens to share with a partner how they can look for a way out of temptations that call them.

Anchor-edge Through Jesus

Theme: Hope

Scripture: Hebrews 6:19a

Summary: Students will interview each other about hope and create "hope anchors."

Preparation: Gather enough self-hardening clay (in at least three different colors) for each student to receive a golf ball-sized ball of clay.

Have students get into pairs, and hand each person in the pair a different color of clay.

Say: **Many things give us hope, such as a good grade, a new friendship, or even seeing a rainbow. Hope is believing that we will be all right or that we have good news in our future. I would like you to take turns being a "Good News" anchor. A news anchor is someone who reports news to other people. Interview your partner and find out something he or she feels hope about, to report to the class. After you've interviewed your partner, let him or her interview you.**

After about three to five minutes, say: **Now give your partner a piece of your clay and interview someone else. After your second interview, give each other a piece of clay as you did with your first partner.**

Allow another few minutes, and then call the kids together to sit in a circle. Ask:

• **What good news did you find that gives your friends hope?**

• **Why is hope important?**

Read aloud Hebrews 6:19a. Then ask:

• **How does your hope in Jesus act like an anchor to your faith?**

Tell the students to take the three pieces of clay they have and roll each piece into a long roll. Show them how to connect the two smaller pieces into a cross and then arc and connect the bottom piece to make an anchor shape with the clay. Hold up a sample anchor that shows the cross at the top and arc at the bottom.

Say: **This anchor shows the cross to remind us of Jesus and that he died for us. The bottom of the anchor is shaped like a smile to remind us of the hope we have because Jesus is now alive in heaven, as we will be one day. We have an edge in this life because we know that Jesus gives us hope. Keep these anchors as a reminder that our faith is anchored in Jesus, who guides and protects us and gives us our hope.**

Covered With Cares

Theme: Handling Tough Times

Scripture: Psalm 55:22

Summary: Students will dress a volunteer in cumbersome clothing to represent tough times. Then they'll learn that letting God carry their cares is like shedding a heavy load.

Preparation: Gather a supply of heavy clothing, including articles of outerwear. You'll want to include a sweater, a winter hat, a scarf, mittens or gloves, a heavy winter coat, and winter boots.

Gather everyone together. Choose one student to be the volunteer and two more to be your assistants. Have all three kids join you in front of the class.

Say: **We're going to use our volunteer here to demonstrate what it's like to be burdened down with cares. For each article of clothing I ask my assistants to dress our volunteer in, I want you to call out a tough time that kids your age have to deal with. Maybe it's peer pressure at school. Or maybe it's worrying about your parents' divorce. Are you ready? Let's dress our volunteer in cares!**

Hold up each piece of clothing you brought, and let kids decide on the tough time it represents. Then let your assistants dress the volunteer in that piece of clothing. Make sure that kids decide on a new care for each article of clothing. Encourage your assistants to ham it up as they dress the volunteer, making comments such as, "How does that feel, nice and heavy?" or "Wow! I can barely see you under all those cares!"

When the volunteer is wearing all of the clothing, lead the class in a round of applause for your assistants; then let them sit down. Ask your volunteer these questions:

- **How do you feel under there, all covered with cares about tough times?**
- **What would make you feel better?**

Then ask the rest of the class these questions:

- **What do you do when you're burdened down by cares in real life?**
- **Who can help you get rid of your cares during tough times?**

Ask a student to read aloud Psalm 55:22 as others follow along in their own Bibles.

Say: **All we have to do when we're covered with cares is give our worries to God. He won't let us fall if we rely on him. Let's unburden our volunteer and relieve him** [or her] **of all these cares.**

Choose two new assistants, and let them help the volunteer remove the clothing. During the process, remind kids that casting our cares on the Lord is a relief, just like shedding cumbersome clothing. We can feel lighter and happier knowing that God is bearing our cares for us.

Unhealthy Weight Gain

Theme: Sin

Scripture: Ezekiel 33:10-11a

Summary: Preteens will pull a "sled" full of kids to represent the weight of sin that we needlessly carry with us.

Preparation: You will need pencils, paper, envelopes, a large sheet of very heavy cardboard, and a jump-rope.

Say: **I want you to think about sin today. Sin is doing something we know is wrong, something that God does not want us to do. I'm handing you a pencil and slip of paper to write down a sin you have committed. After you finish writing, put the paper in an envelope, and seal the envelope so that no one can see it.** Give the kids time to do this.

Then have the students stand in a line facing forward with their envelopes in one of their hands. Pick one preteen to hold the rope in one hand with the envelope in the other. Have the first person in line sit on the front edge of the cardboard and take the other end of the rope. Tell the first preteen to start pulling the seated student past the other students. Tell him that he can stop pulling anytime if he lets go and turns around.

Tell the other kids that as the cardboard passes them, they are to sit on it and hold onto the rope until the preteen who's pulling stops and lets go of the rope. When a student stops his turn pulling, he should join the line at the end, and all the students should get off the cardboard to let another person take a turn pulling the other kids. After several turns, ask:

• **How did it feel the longer you tried to pull on the rope?**

• **Why did you try to keep going when you knew that you could stop pulling at any time?**

Have a volunteer read aloud Ezekiel 33:10-11a while others follow along in their Bibles. Then ask:

• **How does sin weigh us down?**

• **According to this verse, how does God feel about sin?**

• **What does God want you to do with your sins?**

Say: **Sin is a burden that we don't have to carry. Just as in our game, we don't have to keep pulling our sins along with us. God tells us in this verse that he is not happy when people choose to hold onto their sins and die. God is happy when we repent, turn away from our sins, and ask for forgiveness so that we can live.**

Let's pray together and ask God to forgive the sins that are written inside our envelopes. We can then rip the envelopes up and throw them away because we know that God will forgive us and that we don't have to carry around the weight of that sin any longer.

Lead the kids in prayer, asking forgiveness for sins and God's help to keep us from repeating our sins. Have them rip the envelopes and throw them away.

Eternal Life in Your Hands

Theme: Eternal Life

Scripture: 1 Timothy 6:12

Summary: Preteens will try to collect and hold on to strips of cloth and then discuss how to fight for and hold on to faith.

Preparation: You will need four 12-inch strips of cloth per student, one each of four different colors. If you have a class smaller than eight, use only two colors.

Read aloud 1 Timothy 6:12 while students follow along in their Bibles. Then ask:

- **What does fighting mean in this verse?**
- **Why is it important to fight for faith?**
- **How do you fight to keep your faith?**

Hand each student four different-colored strips of cloth. Tell kids to tuck the strips partially into a pants pocket, at the waist, or from a sleeve or belt loop so that at least half of each strip is visible. Then have kids chase each other, trying to collect only one color of the cloth strips. Each strip they take from another person must be tucked in with the others, making sure it is visible and able to be taken by someone else. Have any students who lose all four strips continue playing until they collect at least one piece of cloth.

After playing for a few minutes, stop and have the kids gather in groups based on the color of the strips they have collected. Put any student with no clear choice in the smallest group. Assign one of the following categories to each group: when they are sad, when they are scared, when they are happy, and when they are angry. Ask groups to brainstorm ways that they need to fight to keep their faith during the time assigned to them. If you have only two colors of cloth, have each group take two of the four categories listed above. Give them about ten minutes to discuss ways to keep their faith. Then call the group together into a circle. Have each group share their ideas with the whole group. Then say: **God's promise of eternal life is so important that we are told in the Bible to hold onto it, to keep our faith no matter what happens. In our game, we had to fight to get and keep our strips of cloth. This was hard work, and you had to really want the strips of cloth in order to get them or to keep them. Eternal life is so much more important than a few pieces of cloth. God wants us to fight the good fight of faith so that we can take hold of and believe in his promises.**

Ask the students to share with a partner one way they will "fight" to keep their faith this week.

A Gift of Love

Theme: God's Love

Scripture: John 3:16

Summary: Kids will analyze John 3:16 as they comprehend the gift God has given us in his Son.

Preparation: You'll need pencils and a photocopy of the "John 3:16" handout (p. 24) for each student.

Say: **Today we're going to talk about God's love. I have a Bible verse for us to read. It's one you may be familiar with.**

Have a volunteer read aloud John 3:16 as others follow along in their Bibles. Then ask kids how many of them already knew the verse.

Say: **Like I said, this is a familiar verse—one that lots of people know or** *think* **they know. But since it pretty much sums up what Christianity is all about, let's look at this verse a little more closely.**

Give each student a pencil and a copy of the "John 3:16" handout. Give kids several minutes to complete the questions. Then have kids form pairs to compare their answers. For each question on the handout, ask volunteers to read their answers to the rest of the class.

Say: **This verse is so amazing because it's so simple and yet so powerful. God was willing to give up Jesus, his only Son, for each person in the world. He wants each person in the world to believe in Jesus so they won't perish, and so they can spend eternity with him in heaven. And all we have to do to receive this incredible, indescribable gift is believe in Jesus. It's so simple! Let's thank God for his love.**

Have kids each write a short prayer to God on the back of their handouts, thanking him for his love and for the gift of Jesus. Encourage kids to take their handouts home to remind them of how much God loves them.

John 3:16

"For God so loved the world that he gave his one and only Son, that whoever believes in him shall not perish but have eternal life."

1. What is your definition of love?

2. How does God's love differ from human love?

3. What is your most valuable possession?

4. Would you be willing to give up that possession for people who may not even like you? Explain.

5. Who are the people you love most in this world?

6. Would you be willing to sacrifice their lives for the sake of people who may not even like you? Why or why not?

7. What does it mean to believe in Jesus?

8. How can your life show that you believe in Jesus?

9. What does this verse imply happens if you don't believe in Jesus?

10. What is your reaction to God's act of love in giving his only Son to die for us so that we can go to heaven? Sum up your reaction in one word.

Can I Help You?

Theme: Serving God

Scripture: Matthew 25:34-40

Summary: Students will be waiters and waitresses in a "Serving God" restaurant.

Preparation: You'll need scrap paper, pencils, a large sheet of poster board, markers, and a few simple food items with necessary utensils and containers to serve the food.

Begin by asking preteens:

• **Have you ever been at a restaurant where you received really good service? Explain.**

• **Have you ever been in a restaurant where you received really poor service? Explain.**

• **What makes the difference between good service and poor service?**

Allergy Alert

Be aware that some children have food allergies that can be dangerous. Know your children, and consult with parents about allergies their children may have. Also be sure to carefully read food labels, as hidden ingredients can cause allergy-related problems.

Say: **Today you're going to have the opportunity to serve each other in our very own "Serving God" restaurant. But first, we must create a menu for our restaurant.**

Have students form pairs. Give each pair a sheet of scrap paper and a pen or pencil. Say: **I'd like you and your partner to brainstorm one item for the menu. The item won't be food—instead, it will be something you can do to serve God by serving others in a restaurant. Think of specific things you might be able to do for other people, and then choose just one and write it on your paper. For example, you might say something like, "Greet them with a smile" or "Listen carefully to their order."**

Have students create and turn in their ideas, and then compile them and write them on the sheet of poster board under the heading "Serving God."

Say: **Now you'll have the opportunity to put your ideas into practice. With your partner, I'd like you to decide who will be the waiter or waitress first.**

Give each server a pen and paper. Show students their food choices, and explain that waiters and waitresses should take their customers' orders using as many of the items on the "Serving God" menu as they can. Have waiters and waitresses serve their customers, and then have them switch roles.

While students are enjoying their snack, ask a volunteer to read aloud Matthew 25:34-40. Ask:

• **What did you learn about good service from the experience you've had here today?**

• **What does the Bible tell you about good service?**

• **How can we use the ideas we've discussed here today in our everyday lives?**

All Things

Theme: Praising God

Scripture: Psalm 148

Summary: Preteens will present a psalm of praise.

Preparation: You'll need art supplies of all kinds, CD player, rhythm instruments, costumes, fabric scraps, and any other creative materials you can find.

Have preteens turn in their Bibles to Psalm 148. Take turns having kids each read a verse aloud until they've read the whole psalm. Then ask:

• **How do you think the sun, moon, and stars could praise God?**

• **How could the sky and rocks praise God?**

• **How could the oceans and sea creatures praise God?**

• **How could the weather praise God?**

• **How can mountains and trees praise God?**

• **How can you praise God?**

After brainstorming together, have the kids form four groups. Assign the first group verses 1-3, the second group verses 4-7, the third group verses 8-9, and the fourth group verses 10-12. In their groups, they should create something to express their verses, using whatever supplies are available. For example, preteens might create a dance, a skit, music, or visual art.

After sufficient time for preparation, call the groups back together. Ask a strong reader to read the psalm aloud, pausing while the small groups present their verses. For verses 13-14, everyone should join together to praise God however they feel comfortable.

If your class is very small, have everyone work together to express the psalm, or assign each person a few verses to work on individually. If your class is large, you could assign each verse to a small group to work on.

Truth in Advertising

Theme: God's Promises

Scripture: Hebrews 10:23

Summary: Kids will evaluate the promises that magazine advertisements make and compare them with the promise God has made to us through Jesus.

Preparation: You'll need at least one magazine for each student. Magazines should contain lots of advertisements. You'll also need paper and pencils.

Gather kids together and say: **I want you to look through these magazines and make a list of all the promises that the advertisements make. For example, one ad might promise whiter teeth, another might promise that you'll lose weight, and another might promise that you'll be more popular if you use their product.**

Give kids about five minutes to list the promises the ads in the magazines make. Then gather everyone together in a circle. Explain that each person will get a chance to stand in the center of the circle and read his or her list of promises. After each promise, the rest of the class will respond with a thumbs-up sign if they believe the promise, and a thumbs-down sign if they don't believe the promise.

After everyone has had a chance to read his or her list, lead kids in a round of applause for everyone's participation.

Say: **I guess it's true—you can't believe everything you read. Lots of these promises sound pretty far-fetched to me. But that's never true with God's promises. Listen to this.**

Have a volunteer read aloud Hebrews 10:23 as kids follows along in their own Bibles. Ask:

• **What *hope* do you think this verse is referring to?**

• **In what ways is God faithful to you?**

Say: **We have the hope of eternal life when we believe in Jesus. That's the hope this verse is referring to. God promised us that if we believe in Jesus, we'll go to heaven. And God never, ever breaks his promises!**

A Holy Helper

Theme: Prayer

Scripture: Romans 8:26-27; 1 Thessalonians 5:17

Summary: Preteens will watch a video clip and discuss prayer.

Preparation: You'll need a TV/VCR and the video *Sister Act*. Before class, cue the video to the scene you'll be showing. When the studio logo appears, set your VCR counter to 0:00:00. Fast forward to approximately 0:21:40, where you'll see Whoopi Goldberg standing in front of a mirror in a nun's habit. This is immediately after the shot of the other nuns at prayer. You'll play through approximately 0:24:27, when the nun says, "Be seated."

Show the video clip to the class. After viewing the clip, lead a discussion about prayer. Ask:

- **What made this scene so funny?**
- **When is it hard for you to pray?**
- **Why do you pray? Where? When?**

Ask the kids to turn to Romans 8:26-27 in their Bibles. Read the verses aloud while kids follow along. Ask:

- **What do these verses tell us about prayer?**
- **How does God help us when we don't know how to pray?**

Now ask preteens to turn to 1 Thessalonians 5:17. Ask a volunteer to read this brief verse aloud. Ask:

- **What do you think it means to pray continually? Is this possible? How?**

Say: **God wants us to be in constant communication with him, and he's given us his Holy Spirit to help us. Let's spend some time now in prayer.**

Let preteens move around the room and get comfortable for a time of guided prayer. When they're ready, open the prayer time.

Pray: **Dear God, we love you and want to pray continually. We don't always know how or what to pray, but we thank you for your Holy Spirit who helps us pray. Hear us now as we praise you for your goodness.** Pause for kids to pray silently.

Hear us now as we thank you for

In general, federal copyright laws do not allow you to use videos (even ones you own) for any purpose other than home viewing. Though some exceptions allow for the use of short segments of copyrighted material for educational purposes, it's best to be on the safe side. Your church can obtain a license from the Motion Picture Licensing Corporation for a small fee. Just visit www.mplc.com or call 1-800-462-8855 for more information. When using a video that is not covered by the license, we recommend directly contacting the movie studio to seek permission for use of the clip.

the many blessings you give us every day. Pause for kids to pray silently.

Hear us now as we pray for those we love. Pause for kids to pray silently.

Hear us now as we pray for the things we need. Pause for kids to pray silently.

Hear us now as we pray for our country and its leaders. Pause for kids to pray silently.

In Jesus' name we pray. Amen.

Ballooning Faith

Theme: Growing in Faith

Scripture: 2 Corinthians 10:15-16a

Summary: Kids will explore how growing faith can help everyone learn about Jesus.

Preparation: You'll need one balloon per student; masking tape; pens; and a large, fuzzy blanket. Use the masking tape to write the letters "w-o-r-l-d" at the top of the blanket.

Have students form pairs and brainstorm ways to grow their faith. Tell each pair to choose its best idea and write it on one uninflated balloon. After they've finished, ask them to brainstorm ways to help *others* grow in faith. Tell each pair to write its best idea on a second balloon.

Say: **We should try to grow in our faith, not only to help ourselves, but also to help others learn about Jesus. These balloons are like our faith because they start small, but they can grow really big. Let's share your ideas for growing your own faith and the faith of others.**

After several students have shared, ask:

• **What ideas can we do together as a class?**

Read aloud 2 Corinthians 10:15-16a, and then hang or drape the blanket in front of the students. Ask them to blow up and tie off their balloons.

Say: **Our Bible verse reminds us that as we grow in our faith we help others as well as ourselves. Let's rub our balloons against our clothes or heads and then stick them onto the blanket. If you cause other balloons to fall off, you must help put them back on. Let's see if we can get everyone's balloon to stick on the blanket at once.**

Have preteens stick their balloons on the blanket, filling the "world" with faith. Then ask:

• **What was the hardest part of this activity? Why?**

• Why is it hard to get all the balloons to stick?

• What's the hardest part of trying to grow in your faith?

Say: It's hard to fill the world with faith, but with God's help our growing faith "rubs off" on others. God uses our growing faith to help others learn about him, and he uses our growing faith to help us get closer to him, too.

Section 2:
Devotions About Friends

Righteous Lips

Theme: Honesty

Scripture: Proverbs 10:32; 12:18-19, 22

Summary: Preteens will view a video clip and talk about lies.

Preparation: You'll need a TV/VCR and the video *Chicken Run*. Before class, cue up the video to the scene you'll be showing. When the studio logo appears, set your VCR counter to 0:00:00. Fast forward to approximately 0:39:28, where you'll see and hear a bell ringing, and you'll hear the words, "Roll call!" Play until approximately 0:43:27, with the scene of the rooftops of the chicken coops.

Show the video clip for your preteens. After the clip, lead a discussion about lying. Ask:

• **What do you think: Should Ginger have told the truth? Why or why not?**

• **When has telling the truth backfired on you?**

• **Is it OK to lie if someone would be hurt by the truth? Explain.**

• **What's the last "white lie" you told? What was the result?**

In general, federal copyright laws do not allow you to use videos (even ones you own) for any purpose other than home viewing. Though some exceptions allow for the use of short segments of copyrighted material for educational purposes, it's best to be on the safe side. Your church can obtain a license from the Motion Picture Licensing Corporation for a small fee. Just visit www.mplc.com or call 1-800-462-8855 for more information. When using a video that is not covered by the license, we recommend directly contacting the movie studio to seek permission for use of the clip.

• **Is it ever OK to lie? Why or why not?**

Have the kids look up Proverbs 12:18-19, 22 in their Bibles, and ask a volunteer to read the verses aloud. Ask:

• **What do these verses tell us about lying?**

• **What about those "reckless words" in verse 18? How can you watch your words so they won't "pierce" anyone "like a sword"?**

• **How can you use your words to bring healing at home? with friends?**

Have the kids turn to Proverbs 10:32, and ask a volunteer to read the verse aloud. Ask:

• **According to this verse, how can you increase your odds of saying the right things?**

In closing, pray together with your students that God will give them wisdom and righteousness to speak words of healing rather than hurt.

Give or Gobble

Theme: Sharing Your Faith

Scripture: John 4:25-30

Summary: Students will make decisions about whether to share or hoard candy randomly distributed.

Preparation: You'll need bags of candy or some special treat your kids would enjoy.

Allergy Alert

Be aware that some children have food allergies that can be dangerous. Know your children, and consult with parents about allergies their children may have. Also be sure to carefully read food labels, as hidden ingredients can cause allergy-related problems.

When students arrive, be nibbling on a snack you've brought, but don't offer any to your class. After a few minutes of torment, offer lots of candy to only a handful of your students and observe their response—will they share or hoard? Finally offer the goodies to everyone, and spend a few minutes sharing as you chow down. Ask:

• **How does it feel when someone should share, but you know they're holding out on you?**

• **Why do we get selfish sometimes when we have more than enough?**

Say: **Unfortunately, that's often the way we treat the gospel. We aren't willing to share the good news. There's plenty for everyone, but too often we hold out, keeping all of God's grace and goodness to ourselves. Sometimes we decide just who we should and shouldn't share with—people we think will be "receptive" or those who would make "good Christians."**

Ask a volunteer or two to read aloud John 4:1-30. Ask:

- **Why did most people avoid this woman?**
- **Why did Jesus reach out to her?**
- **How did she respond to the grace Jesus offered her?**
- **What did she do when she heard the good news? What did you do?**

Say: **Sharing your faith can be a scary thing, especially if you're shy or just learning what to say. But practice helps.**

To close, give students an opportunity to practice sharing their faith with classmates by rehearsing what they could say, questions to answer, or different scenarios that might arise. Encourage them to use the Bible text as a pattern or to brainstorm their own ways to strike up a conversation with someone about God.

Taming the Tongue

Theme: Gossip

Scripture: James 3:3-8

Summary: Kids will compare trying to control a remote-control car to trying to control their tongues from gossiping.

Preparation: You'll need a working remote-control car and objects with which to set up a simple obstacle course or track for the car.

Gather kids together in a large, uncarpeted room or outdoors. If you meet outdoors, be sure to have plenty of adult supervision. Show kids the remote-control car you brought.

Say: **I'm going to give each of you a chance to try to control this car. But first we have to set up a little obstacle course.**

Have kids help you set up the obstacle course. You could set cones or buckets in a line for the car to swerve around, or you could set up a track. Give each student a chance to run the car once through the obstacle course. If you have a large class, have kids work in teams with one operator and the rest cheerleaders. After each person has had a turn, dismantle the course and meet inside. Ask:

- **Was it easy or hard to control the car? Why?**
- **Why didn't the car "obey" your every command?**

Say: **This remote-control car reminds me of something the Bible says about our tongues. Let's find out more.**

Have kids form pairs and read James 3:3-8 with their partners. Then have partners discuss the following questions. After each question, invite volunteers to share their answers with the rest of the class. Ask:

• **How is the tongue like the remote-control car in our activity?**

• **What kind of trouble do our tongues get us in to?**

• **One way our tongues betray is by gossiping; what kind of damage does gossip do?**

• **Has gossip ever hurt you or someone you know? What was that like?**

• **What can you do this week to control your tongue and keep from gossiping?**

Say: **Just as our remote-control car kept going out of control, gossip can get out of control just as easily. It may start with a little word behind someone's back, and before you know it, there are rumors flying all over the place. That's one reason it's so important for us to control our tongues. We can do great damage and cause deep hurt by letting our tongues gossip. Let's commit to trying to control our tongues this week. Next time we meet, we'll compare notes about how successful we were.**

Add the Bad

Theme: Forgiving Others

Scripture: Matthew 18:21-35

Summary: An object lesson will get students thinking about forgiveness. Then a number-crunching exercise will help everyone realize just how much God has forgiven us.

Preparation: You'll need a loaded squirt gun and one or two prearranged volunteers from class. Have paper, pencils, and a calculator or two on hand.

> **Please be sure that the squirt gun is obviously a toy**—don't use one that looks like a real weapon.

Before your class meets, privately ask one or two good-natured students to help you with a discussion about forgiveness. Be sure they sit near the front of the room and don't mind getting wet.

When students arrive, repeatedly squirt your secret volunteers with the squirt gun, apologizing insincerely between shots. After several hits, ask the class:

• **Why is it sometimes so hard to forgive?**

• **Do you think there should be a limit to how many times we have to forgive somebody? Explain.**

Have students form groups of three to five. Ask them to read Matthew 18:21-35 in their groups. Give paper and a pencil to each small group. Ask the

Trash Talk

Theme: Harmful Words
Scripture: Proverbs 15:1; James 3:9-10
Summary: Kids will learn that harmful words are powerful and can't be taken back.
Preparation: None needed.

Say: **Sometimes when we're hurt or angry, we lash out at people with harmful words.** Ask kids to share a story about a time when they were hurt or angry and they lashed out in this way.

God has some advice for us in these situations. But first, let's look at what he says about harmful words.

Ask a volunteer to read aloud James 3:9-10. Say: **The Bible tells us that praising and cursing should not come out of the same mouth. Cursing can mean using swear words, but it also means any harmful words that make others feel bad. If you've ever said a swear word, stick your left thumb in your mouth.**

Be honest here—stick your own left thumb in your mouth! This will encourage the kids to be honest as well. You may have to remove your thumb briefly while you continue the discussion. Say: **Now let's all say, "Praise you, Jesus!"** Pause.

If you've ever said something that hurt someone else, put your right thumb in your mouth too. Say, "Praise you, Jesus." Pause.

If you've ever been hurt by someone else's words, put three more fingers in your mouth and say, "Praise you, Jesus." Pause.

I couldn't understand you! Now take your fingers and thumbs out of your mouth. Ask:

- **How did our praises sound with the fingers and thumbs in our mouths?**
- **How is this like what happens when we use harmful words?**

Say: **Harmful words tear people apart and mess things up. That's why God doesn't want us to use our mouths for harmful words. Once they're said, the damage is done. You can't take them back. Now let's see what God's advice is for us when we are hurt, angry, or feel like fighting with someone.**

Invite a student to read aloud Proverbs 15:1 while others follow in their Bibles. Say: **God says that if we use gentle words instead of harsh and mean ones, it will help turn away the anger.** Ask:

- **Is it possible to use a soft word when we're mad? Why or why not?**
- **How will living out this Scripture affect your friendships?**

• How have your harmful words torn others down? Explain.

• How have your gentle words turned away anger? Explain.

Close by having kids brainstorm ways they could use a gentle answer to the situations they mentioned at the beginning of class that made them angry.

Signs of the Times

Theme: Judging Others

Scripture: Matthew 7:3-5

Summary: Preteens will experience what it's like to see others' faults without being able to see their own.

Preparation: On separate sheets of paper, create signs that express fictitious faults. You'll need one sign for each person in class and tape. If you have a large class, duplicate several of the signs. Make sure the signs are silly, not hurtful. For example, the signs could say, "Eats with toes," "Used to eat dirt as a kid," and "Likes to sing off-key in the shower."

Have kids line up shoulder to shoulder with their backs to you. Tape one of the papers you prepared before class onto each student's back. Then have kids turn around to face you.

Say: **Now you can mill around the room and look at what's written on everyone else's back. But don't tell anyone what his or her sign says, OK? Start milling!**

Give kids a minute or two to read what's written on the signs taped to everyone else's backs. Then have kids take off their signs and sit in a circle on the floor. Ask:

• **What was it like to be able to read what was written on others' signs?**

• **What was it like not being able to see what was written on your own sign?**

Say: **In this activity, there were things that were obvious about others because we could read their signs. But we couldn't tell what was written on our own backs. That's kind of how it is when we judge others. It's easy to see and judge other people's faults, but it's a lot harder to recognize our own. Let's see what the Bible has to say about judging others.**

Have kids form pairs and read together Matthew 7:3-5. Then have partners discuss these questions. Ask pairs to share their answers with the rest of the class.

• **How does this passage remind you of the activity we just did?**

• **How can you keep from judging others?**

Say: **It's so easy to judge others without paying attention to our own faults. Perhaps one way to stop doing that is to ask ourselves if we're without faults every time we are tempted to judge someone else. That should remind us of what the Bible says. Let's try it!**

Two Are Better Than One

Theme: Being a Friend

Scripture: Ecclesiastes 4:9-12

Summary: Preteens will try to stand alone and with a friend, then try to break cords of one and three strands. Then they'll talk about being a friend.

Preparation: You'll need pieces of yarn, approximately three feet long, four pieces per pair of kids.

Begin class by having the students sit down with their backs against a wall. Keeping their backs against the wall and without using their hands, they must try to stand up. After a few minutes of trying this—most unsuccessfully— have students form pairs. Explain that partners should sit on the floor, back to back, and link arms. Again they should try to stand up, keeping their backs together. Most pairs should be able to do this. Then ask:

• **Which way were you able to stand up? Why?**

• **How is that like friendship?**

• **When have you needed a friend in your life to help you up or to help you in another way?**

Next, distribute a piece of yarn to each pair. Explain that preteens should try to break the yarn. Most students will be able to do this.

Now distribute three new pieces of yarn to each pair. Demonstrate how one partner should hold one end of all the yarn, while the other braids the strings together. If you have any kids that like to braid, invite them to lead the demonstration. When kids have finished braiding, have them try again to break the now-braided yarn. Then ask:

• **How were you able to break the yarn? Why?**

• **How is that like friendship?**

Read aloud Ecclesiastes 4:9-12. Ask:

• **How did our activities illustrate this passage?**

• **According to this passage, what are some good reasons to be a friend** and to have a friend?

In closing, have each pair join with another pair to form groups of four. In their small groups, they should talk about this question:

• **How can you become a better friend?**

A Little Help for Your Friends

Theme: Helping Hurting Friends

Scripture: 1 Peter 3:8

Summary: After joining their voices together in song, kids will brain-storm ways to live in harmony and help their hurting friends.

Preparation: You'll need an index card and a pencil for each student.

Say: **Let's see what kind of voices you have today!**

Lead kids in singing "Row, Row, Row Your Boat" or another song that can be sung in a round. Sing the song through together once, and then have kids form groups and sing the song in a round.

Explain that groups can now add another element to the song, such as sound effects and beats. Kids can stomp their feet, clap their hands, or slap their thighs to accompany the singing. Have kids sing the song as a round again, this time adding the sound effects. After the "concert," lead the group in a round of applause for their efforts.

Say: **We may not win a Grammy, but we did pretty well working together to create a harmonious performance! Let's talk a little about harmony.** Ask:

• **We all know what harmony means in music, but what do you think it means to *live* in harmony?**

• **What kinds of things sometimes keep us from living in harmony with each other?**

Say: **Sometimes it's hard to live in harmony with others. We can get so caught up in our own concerns, that we may not be sensitive to the needs of others around us. The Bible gives us some good advice about how to live in harmony. Here's what it says.**

Have a student read aloud 1 Peter 3:8 as others follow along in their Bibles. Ask:

• **What four ways does this verse tell us we can live in harmony?**

• **Which of these is hardest for you to do? Why?**

Say: **People are hurting all around us—even our friends. To help them, we just need to follow the advice of this verse in four ways. We need to be sym-pathetic when those near us are having problems; we need to love others like** we love our families; we need to show compassion for friends who are hurting; and we need to be humble and not think we're better than others. Let's think about how we can put this into practice.

Have kids form four groups, and assign each group one of the four ways to live in harmony. Each group should think of one situation in which they could demonstrate that way to help their hurting friends. For example, kids might say that they can be sympathetic when a friend is upset about a family problem, rather than avoiding that friend. Or kids might say they can show compassion for the unpopular new student by sitting with the student at lunch.

After a few minutes, have each group pantomime their situation for the rest of the class. See if the other groups can guess how to help a hurting friend. Encourage kids to follow through on their helpful intentions this week!

That's Not Fair!

Theme: Overcoming Prejudice

Scripture: Romans 12:14-18

Summary: Students will experience unfair discrimination and then discover how to handle prejudice in their own lives.

Preparation: Set up a simple snack on a table. You'll need only enough for a small group of students; however, have enough snacks set aside so that all of the students can have some later.

Allergy Alert
Be aware that some children have food allergies that can be dangerous. Know your children, and consult with parents about allergies their children may have. Also be sure to carefully read food labels, as hidden ingredients can cause allergy-related problems.

As students arrive, divide them into two groups according to clothing color. You can choose the colors as they arrive, but you'll need to have one fairly small group and one larger group. Have the students in the smaller group sit in chairs around a table; have the other group stand against one wall.

Say: **If you're sitting in a chair at the table, you may go ahead and eat your snack. If you're standing against the wall, you'll just need to wait for them to finish.**

If students protest or ask what's going on, don't give them much explanation; just repeat your instructions. When the students at the table have finished eating, have all students sit down, and give snacks to those who didn't get them before. Ask:

• **What just happened here?**

• **How do you think I chose who got to eat first?**

• **Do you think that was fair? Why or why not?**

• **Those of you who ate first, how did you feel as you were eating your snack? Explain.**

• **Those of you who were standing against the wall, how did you feel as you watched others eat their snacks? Explain.**

• **Have you ever had an experience like this in real life? Has someone ever left you out or been mean to you because of how you looked? Explain.**

• **What do you think you should do when someone treats you badly?**

Ask a volunteer to read aloud Romans 12:14-18. Ask:

• **What does this passage tell you about what to do when someone treats you badly?**

• **Do you think this will be easy or difficult to do this week? Explain.**

Say: **Let's practice some of these ideas.** Have students form pairs. Ask each pair to think of a situation in which one person might treat another unkindly. Once pairs have thought of their situations, have them brainstorm ways they might follow the Scripture in this situation. For example, the person being treated unkindly might just give the other person a friendly smile and move on. Have pairs take turns role-playing the unkind person and the "victim," and encourage them to apply the principles from Romans as they respond.

To close, pray with the group together, asking God to help each person respond with love and kindness when they are treated unfairly or unkindly.

Two-Way Faith

Theme: Conflicts Between Faith and Friendship

Scripture: Psalm 118:8; John 17:20-21

Summary: Preteens will play two different games of tag and learn how to share their faith with their friends.

Preparation: You'll need a large, open space and masking tape. Before class, use the tape to mark a line near one end of the room as a "safe base."

Have all the students except one line up behind the safe-base line. Instruct the one student to turn his back to the class. Tell the rest of the class that they are to try to sneak up behind that person and tag him before he turns around, chases, and tags them. If someone can tag that student, he becomes the new "It." But if "It" manages to tag someone before he returns across the "safe" line, that person must join "It" so that play resumes with two people as "It." Play for a few rounds, and then ask a volunteer to read aloud Psalm 118:8. Ask:

- **Why does the Bible tell us to trust in God rather than man?**
- **How can trusting our friends instead of God lead to trouble?**
- **What would happen if you had to stand up for Jesus against your friends?**
- **When are some times we might be excluded by our friends because of Jesus?**

Say: **Sometimes our friends might ask us to turn our backs on God, but the Bible tells us that God is the only one who is safe to trust all the time. Our game of tag reminds us that friends might try to lure us away from the safety of following Jesus. Let's read another passage together.**

Ask a volunteer to read aloud John 17:20-21. Then play a different tag game. One person is "It" until a second person is tagged. They join hands and keep tagging people to join them, until everyone is tagged. Play a few rounds and then sit down together. Ask:

- **How was this game of tag different from the first one?**
- **Why might you *want* to be tagged in this game?**
- **When are some times we can include our friends so that they can learn more about Jesus' love? Will you include someone this week? Who?**

Say: **In this game of tag, we tried to include more and more people, instead of playing against each other. There are ways we can include our friends so that they learn more about Jesus. Jesus wants us to trust him and to show our friends why we trust him. We know that sometimes our friends might not want us to trust Jesus instead of them, but Jesus wants everyone to become his friend so that one day we can all be one with him.**

You Know Me...and You Love Me

Theme: Self-Image

Scripture: Psalm 139:1-18, 23-24

Summary: Students will discover and experience God's amazing love for each of his precious creatures.

Preparation: Set up the following stations around your room. If possible, you might want to use a larger area so that students will have room to spread out. Photocopy the "You Know Me...and You Love Me" handout (p. 45), one per student, and cut the copies on the cut lines. Distribute the sections to the appropriate stations. You may also want to have a CD player and a CD of soft, reflective, worshipful music to play as students move through these stations.

Station 1: You'll need Bibles and plenty of warm, soft blankets.

Station 2: You'll need Bibles, paper, tape, and markers.

Station 3: You'll need Bibles, small mirrors, paper, and pencils.

Station 4: You'll need Bibles, a container of sand, and small jars with lids.

As students arrive, have them be seated. Ask:

• **What is self-image?**

• **You don't have to answer this question aloud, but I want you to think about it. Do you think you have a good self-image or a poor self-image? Why?**

• **What kind of self-image do you think God wants you to have?**

If possible, it would be a good idea to have an adult volunteer at each station to both model the activity and help students understand what they need to do at each station.

Say: **God wants you to have a good self-image, to think positively of yourself because he made you in his image and he loves you more than you can ever know or understand, no matter what. Today we're going to experience the power and wonder of God's image in you through a series of stations.** Show students each of the stations, and explain briefly the process described below. Ask students to approach this activity with a worshipful attitude.

Divide students into four groups to start, but explain that they are to move through the stations individually, not as groups. Give them sufficient time to get through all of the stations. If some finish early, have them sit quietly. When everyone is finished, have students sit comfortably and close their eyes.

Say: **Through these experiences, you've learned that God created you in his own image. He knows everything about you, even the really bad stuff, and he loves you no matter what, just because you're his. Right now, I'd like to read you the end of Psalm 139.** Read aloud Psalm 139:23-24.

Because God loves us so much, he wants to get even closer to us. Sometimes things stand in the way, though. Those things are our own sins and anxious or selfish thoughts. We need to let God search us and know us and help us to get rid of the things that stand in the way of a closer relationship with him. Right now, I'd like you to think of God's enormous, warm, loving light shining down on you and through you. Feel it fill you with warmth and light. Open up every part of yourself to this light...don't hold anything back. Pause. **Think of the dark, small, yucky parts of yourself that you don't think you want anyone to see, especially God.** Pause. **Now imagine God gently, lovingly plucking**

You Know Me...and You Love Me

Station 1

Read Psalm 139:1-6 silently. Think about how well God knows you; he knows everything there is to know about you. Wrap yourself in a blanket and imagine God's warm love "hemming you in," keeping you warm, and touching every part of you.

Station 2

Read Psalm 139:7-12 silently. Think of a time you've tried to hide from God. Maybe you did something you were really ashamed of, or maybe you felt like God had abandoned you. Draw a picture to represent this time and how you felt. Then read the Scripture again. What does it say about God? Can you ever hide from God? God is always with you, no matter what. Take this picture with you. Draw a second picture about God being with you. Tape this picture to the wall.

Station 3

Read Psalm 139:13-16 silently. What does this passage tell you about the way you were created? Sometimes you may not feel so good about your body or the way you look. Look at yourself in a mirror. As you look, think about the fact that God created you exactly the way you are, and he loves every part of you. Write a brief letter to God, thanking him for creating and loving every part of you, even the parts you're not always so happy about. Take this letter with you.

Station 4

Read Psalm 139:17-18 silently. God's thoughts of you and the things he created are more numerous than all of the grains of sand in the universe; there's no way we could count them all. Take a jar and scoop up some sand. As you do, think about how much God loves you to think so many thoughts about you.

those parts out. He sets them aside and fills the spaces with more of his warm, wonderful, loving light. Pause. Take a moment to say "Thank you" to God for knowing you and loving you and bringing you closer to him.

Stick to Your Word

Theme: Keeping Promises

Scripture: Numbers 30:2

Summary: Kids will weave "promise squares" to remind them that broken promises affect us in many ways.

Preparation: You'll need markers, rubber bands, and six wooden craft sticks per student.

Ask:

• **What is a promise or a vow?**

• **What are some promises you have made?**

• **What happens if you break a promise?**

Ask a volunteer to read aloud Numbers 30:2 while others follow along in their Bibles. Distribute craft sticks, six per student. Ask the kids to write their names on the first stick. Tell them to think of promises they have made and to write one on each of the other five sticks. Direct the students to lay three sticks vertically and parallel to each other. Have them weave the other three sticks over and under the first three, starting at the top and weaving the opposite way with the middle stick. Tell them to weave the last stick over and under carefully so that it does not break.

Then ask:

• **How many promises written on your sticks are broken promises?**

• **How can breaking one promise affect the other promises you make?**

Tell the students to hold their promise weavings carefully and then throw them to the ground as hard as possible. Have them stand apart or take turns tossing their squares so that the flying sticks do not hit anyone. Then ask:

• **How does a broken promise affect other people?**

• **How does it affect our relationship with God?**

• **Why should we keep our promises?**

Say: **Even one broken promise affects the other promises. It affects your good name, the people around you, and your relationship with God.**

Let the kids gather their own sticks, and hand them rubber bands to bundle them together. Close with a prayer asking God to help us keep our promises and forgive us when we don't.

The Award Goes to...

Theme: Setting a Good Example

Scripture: Matthew 5:14-16; Philippians 2:14-18

Summary: Students will create "good example" awards for people in their lives.

Preparation: You'll need one sheet of nice parchment paper for each student, gold or silver ribbon or cord, scissors, scratch paper, and fine-tipped markers. To create more of an awards-ceremony feel, you may want to have some or all of the following: a CD player, regal-sounding music, an applause track, an elaborately decorated "throne" or podium, and various other festive decorations, such as balloons and streamers.

Before the devotion, create your own award for someone who has been a good example for you, and be prepared to share the award and the story behind it with students.

This devotion can be as simple or as elaborate as you choose. For the best, most meaningful results, you may want to have your students identify their "good examples" a week ahead of time and issue formal invitations to the ceremony. Then during the ceremony, each award winner can accept the award in person and maybe even say a few words to the group about his or her good example.

Ask preteens:

• **What does it mean to be a good example to others?**

Ask a volunteer to read aloud Matthew 5:14-16; have another volunteer read aloud Philippians 2:14-18. Then ask:

• **What do these passages tell us about being good examples to others?**

• **Who do you know that has been a good example to you? Who would you say has shone like a star in the universe? Who has inspired you to become the best you can be?**

Say: **Today we're going to take some time to recognize those people who have been good examples to us. We might choose to recognize a parent who always guides us in the right direction, or a friend at school who stood up for** what's right even though he or she was made fun of. Take a moment to think of the person you would like to honor for being a good example to you.

Give each person a sheet of scratch paper, a sheet of parchment paper, and some fine-tipped markers. Say: **Now I'd like you to create an award for the person you've chosen. Show your sample award. On your award, I'd like you to include the person's name, why he or she is a good example to you and others, and one of the Bible verses we read today. I've provided scratch paper so that you can sketch your award first, before you put it on nice paper. You can decorate your award if you'd like. When you're thinking of the reasons you're giving this person an award, I'd like you to be as specific and as detailed as possible.**

Give students some time to think and create. When they've finished, have students roll their parchment sheets, and give each student a piece of ribbon or cord to tie the parchment with. Then ask volunteers to share the awards they've created and the stories behind them with the class. If you've chosen to have an awards ceremony, have each student come up, call his or her award winner up to the throne or the podium, and read the award aloud to the winner and the audience. Be sure to play the regal music when the award winner is coming to the stage and leaving the stage, and encourage the audience to clap along with the applause track.

After you've shared the awards, ask:

• **What have you learned from these people about being good examples?**

• **How can you take their good examples and use them to be good examples to others?**

Second-Place Self

Theme: Putting Friends First

Scripture: John 15:12-14

Summary: Kids will use improvisational theater to express ways that they can put friends first.

Preparation: You'll need a variety of objects such as toys, clothes, books, kitchen utensils, and cans of food.

Divide the kids into groups of three to five, and have them read John 15:12-14 in their groups. Ask them to discuss with their group the meaning of *friendship.*

Call the class back together to share their ideas about friendship. Ask:

• **What does it mean to lay down your life for your friend?**

• **Which people might God consider our friends that we might not?**

Tell the students to get back into their groups, and hand each group an item. Ask them to make up a scene to perform for the rest of the class that shows how they could put a friend first, using their given items. Examples you might give include sharing a toy, letting a friend borrow a book, teaching a friend how to cook, or letting them sample a recipe first.

After all the groups have presented their scenes, say: **Jesus laid down his life for us. And he tells us that if we follow his example, we are his friends.** Ask:

• **What did you learn from each other today?**

Tell the kids to pick one idea from the scenes to try out on a friend this week. Ask them to report back the results of this "homework" assignment.

Section 3:
Devotions About Families

Say It With Signs

Theme: Communication

Scripture: Ephesians 4:29

Summary: Kids will create street signs to remind them to follow the Bible's directions when communicating with family members.

Preparation: You'll need paper, pencils, construction paper or poster board, and colorful markers for kids to share.

Give each person a sheet of paper and a pencil. Tell kids they'll have thirty seconds to write the names of all the people they generally communicate with every day. After thirty seconds, tell kids to circle the names of those people who are family members.

Say: **When I asked you to write the names of the people you communicate with every day, I bet a lot of you wrote the names of your friends. That's fine. But I bet some of you might have forgotten to write down all of your family members' names. Sometimes we just take our family members for granted. But they need our attention just as much as—if not more than—anyone else!** Ask:

• **Is it always easy for you to communicate with your family members? Why or why not?**

• **What could you do to make communication in your family better?**

Say: **The Bible's always a good place to look when you want directions about how to improve a situation. Let's see what the Bible says about communication.**

Have a volunteer read aloud Ephesians 4:29 as others follow along in their Bibles.

Say: **I wonder, do you always follow the directions this verse gives when you communicate with your family? I know I don't always live up to this verse. Let's make something to remind us about how God wants us to communicate with our families. Since we look to the Bible for direction, let's make street signs to remind us of this verse.**

Let kids make any kind of street sign they choose. For example, a student might make a stop sign that says, "STOP all unwholesome talk." Another student's sign might say, "CONSTRUCTION SITE: Building Up of Others in Progress."

When kids have finished making their signs, let them display them to each other. Then encourage kids to take their signs home and hang them in their rooms to remind them to follow the Bible's directions for communicating with their families.

Sweet 'n' Sticky

Theme: Obeying Parents

Scripture: Colossians 3:20

Summary: Kids will name "sticky" situations in which they have to obey while making designs with corn syrup and food coloring. They will learn that obedience, while sometimes sticky to learn, feels and tastes good afterward, and above all, pleases the Lord.

Preparation: You'll need a piece of poster board or cardboard for each student, light corn syrup, food coloring, and moist towelettes.

Food coloring stains—fingertips, clothing, carpet—so be careful and prepared!

Ask a volunteer to read aloud Colossians 3:20 while others read along in their Bibles. Then ask:

• **Is it easy or hard for you to live out this Scripture? Explain.**

Pour some corn syrup onto a piece of poster board and touch it, showing kids that it's sticky. Say: **Sometimes obeying our parents is hard to do. We might find ourselves in "sticky" situations where we have to decide if we're going to obey or not. For example, maybe your parents trust you at home alone after school, but you're not supposed to use the phone. Someone at school that you've been wanting for a friend says they'll call you. You have to decide whether to obey your parents and risk having the person think you're** a baby, or disobey your parents and talk to the friend. That's a sticky situation. Tell us about a sticky situation in which you had to choose whether or not to obey.

Give kids time to share. Then give each one a piece of poster board and pour some corn syrup onto each one. Have kids spread the corn syrup out with their fingers while they silently talk to God about when it's hard for them to obey. Then have them add a few drops of food coloring to the corn syrup, blending the colors with their fingers.

Say: **As you spread the colors, make a design and tell God that you want to please him by obeying your parents. Ask him to help you.**

Give kids several minutes to finish making their designs. Then say: **Obeying is sometimes sticky, and we might get into messes, but it pleases the Lord when we obey. And guess what—it's sweet and good for us too!** Have kids taste the syrup on their hands. **Let's remember to please God this week by obeying our parents.**

Set the designs aside to dry. It will take several days, but the designs will dry bright and shiny. Pass out moist towelettes for kids to clean their hands.

Bundle Course

Theme: Getting Along With Siblings

Scripture: Genesis 45:1-5, 22-24

Summary: Students will run through an obstacle course together and talk about getting along with siblings. Prepare carefully and maximize safety!

Preparation: You'll need to set up a simple obstacle course using chairs, a jump-rope, balloons, cones or small boxes, a six-foot long 2x4 board, a nearby staircase, and a darkened closet or classroom. You'll also need lots of duct tape and a pair of scissors.

Set up five stations as follows, each with a sign indicating its name. For "The Pit," tie a jump-rope to two chairs to create a line each team must pass under. For "Slaves' Slalom," use cones or boxes to create a tight course that students must quickly weave through. At "Potiphar's Pass," create a balance beam by securing a 2x4 to the ground with duct tape. For "The Dungeon," place several inflated balloons in a nearby dark closet or classroom. Each group will find and pop one balloon in the dark. Create a climbing activity for the last station, "King of the Mountain." Use a simple staircase or add some panache with a mountain of mattresses. The goal: Get the entire group up and over!

When students arrive, have them form teams of three to six, depending on your class size. Use duct tape to secure team members together—how is up to you, but make sure each team moves as a unit. And be sure to tape only *over* clothing!

Show teams the different stations and have them quickly move through each. Start teams at different stations and all rotate the same direction so no team is kept waiting for long. When teams have finished but are still joined together, ask:

- **What are the good and bad sides of togetherness?**
- **Do you ever feel bound this way to your siblings? Like for better or worse, you are stuck with them? Explain.**

Separate students. Note the signs at each station, and let students make guesses about what the signs had in common. When someone suggests that they were events in the life of Joseph, ask your students to find Genesis 45 in their Bibles. Have a volunteer read aloud verses 1-5 and 22-24.

Say: **Talk about family squabbles! Joseph's brothers were so jealous and annoyed by him that they actually sold him as a slave and told his father he was dead!** Ask:

- **How did Joseph respond to his brothers when he saw them years later?**
- **What things drive you crazy about your brothers and sisters?**
- **What can you do to try to get along with them better this week?**
- **What things do you enjoy about your siblings?**

Close in prayer, thanking God for brothers and sisters—those who are related by blood, and those connected by the blood of Christ.

Recipe for Unity

Theme: Unity in the Family

Scripture: Proverbs 17:1; Romans 15:5-6

Summary: Kids will create recipes for family unity and eat the results.

Preparation: You'll need pencils, index cards, paper plates, graham crackers, icing, candies, sprinkles, peanut butter,

Allergy Alert

Be aware that some children have food allergies that can be dangerous. Know your children, and consult with parents about allergies their children may have. Also be sure to carefully read food labels, as hidden ingredients can cause allergy-related problems.

and plastic knives for each student.

Have kids close their eyes while you read aloud Proverbs 17:1. Then have kids open their eyes, and ask:

- **What images did this verse bring to your mind?**
- **What do you think this verse means?**
- **What is family unity?**
- **Why is it better to starve as a family than feast as enemies?**

Hand each preteen an index card and a pencil. Allow the students to work in small groups to come up with their own "recipes" for family unity. Remind them to list ingredients such as love and sharing, and tell how to make this recipe by writing out each step needed.

When kids are finished, have them share their recipes with the whole group. Then ask:

- **What ingredients did everyone use in their recipe for family unity?**
- **What steps were alike in our recipes?**
- **What can you do to help your family get along together?**

Make available the food ingredients you've brought. Tell kids to pretend to make their recipes using the real food. Ask them to share with a partner which food item equals which ingredient. While kids eat their snacks, say: **This activity helps us remember that it's better to go hungry in a happy family than to feast with a fighting family.**

> **Some healthier,** alternative foods include matzo, spreadable cheese or honey, raisins, and apple chunks.

Read aloud Romans 15:5-6 as a closing prayer.

Different Families, Same Love

Theme: Living With One Parent

Scripture: Exodus 2:1-10; 1 Samuel 1; 1 Kings 17:7-24; Matthew 1:18-25; 13:55-56

Summary: Students will explore different types of biblical families.

Preparation: You'll need copies of the "Different Families, Same Love" handout (p. 56) and pencils.

Begin by having students brainstorm as many different kinds of families as they can think of—they might list families with two parents, single-parent families, families in which grandparents raise their grandchildren, foster families, and so on.

Say: **These families all seem quite different from one another, but there are some things they all have in common.** Ask:

- **What do you think all of these families have in common?**

Say: **One thing all of these types of families have in common is love—the love parents or grandparents or foster parents have for their children, and the love children have for their parents or parental figures.**

Give each student a "Different Families, Same Love" handout (p. 56), and have students number off from one to four. Have all of the "ones" get together, and assign them to read and respond to Scenario 1; have all the "twos" get together and read and respond to Scenario 2; and so on. Give groups some time to read and discuss.

When they've finished, have students form new groups. The new groups should include one person from each of the four original groups. Have students share with these groups what they learned.

When they're finished, say: **You've learned about some people in the Bible who came from different family situations.** Ask:

- **How do you think God views these people and their families?**

Say: **As we can see from these Bible stories, God loves people from all different backgrounds and family situations, and God can use people from many different backgrounds and family situations, too. No matter what your family looks like, you know that your parent or parent figures love you very much and want the best for you. And God loves you, too.**

Different Families, Same Love

Scenario 1

Moses

Read Exodus 2:1-10 and discuss the following questions:

• What was Moses' family situation like?

• Who did Moses grow up with? Why?

• How do you think God felt about Moses and his family?

Scenario 2

Samuel

Read 1 Samuel 1 and discuss the following questions:

• What was Samuel's family situation like?

• Who did Samuel grow up with? Why?

• How do you think God felt about Samuel and his family?

Scenario 3

The Widow's Son

Read 1 Kings 17:7-24 and discuss the following questions:

• What was the boy's family situation like?

• Who did the boy grow up with? Why?

• How do you think God felt about the boy and his family?

Scenario 4

Jesus

Read Matthew 1:18-25; 13:55-56 and discuss the following questions:

• What was Jesus' family situation like?

• Who did Jesus grow up with? Why?

• How do you think God felt about Jesus and his family?

Family Harmonies

Theme: Living in a Blended Family

Scripture: Matthew 12:48-50

Summary: Kids will create music to show the similarities and differences in each family.

Preparation: You'll need paper; pencils; and musical instruments such as bells, kazoos, whistles, rattles, and a drum.

Have a volunteer read aloud Matthew 12:48-50 while others follow along in their Bibles. Then ask:

• **How do you think Jesus' family felt to hear Jesus say this?**

• **How do you think people who wanted to be part of Jesus' family felt to hear this verse?**

• **What do you think this verse means for how you live this week?**

Hand the kids each a piece of paper and a pencil. Ask them to write the names of all their family members on the top, left to right, including their own names as well. Tell them to share the names of their family members with a partner. Then ask:

• **Who did you list in your family?**

• **How was your list the same as your partner's list?**

• **How was your list different from your partner's list? Why?**

Say: **Our families are different from each other in many ways. Some families are blended together into new families when parents remarry or kids live with grandparents. Each family is important, and each member is an important part of his or her family. I want you to draw a heart under the name of each adult in your family. This is to remind you that your family loves you. now draw a star under each child's name. This is to remind you that you are all special to each other. now we're going to create family songs based on the hearts and stars you've drawn.**

Have one student beat the drum in a continuous, steady beat. Tell the other kids that they are going to play long notes for the hearts on their papers—counting in their heads to four beats—and short notes for the stars—counting in their heads just two beats. Lead kids in playing practice heart and star notes.

Select one person to come forward with his or her family "music" and lead the class in playing that music. Allow each preteen to hear his or her family's music, taking turns conducting and playing the various instruments.

Say: **God wants us to know that we are loved and that we are called to** show love in our families. Even though our families may be different, we are grateful God has given us families. Our families may change, but we are to "keep the beat," knowing that we are always part of God's family.

Marble Mania

Theme: Encouraging Family Members

Scripture: Hebrews 10:24

Summary: Kids will use one marble to move another across a finish line. Then they'll discuss how they can encourage family members toward love and good deeds.

Preparation: Before or during the activity, use masking tape to mark a starting line and a finish line on opposite sides of your room. Gather everyone near the starting line. Give each student a marble.

Say: **Let's pretend that this marble is a member of your family. See that finish line over there? Your family member really wants to get there. Maybe the finish line represents a new job your dad wants. Or maybe it represents passing a course your sister is having trouble with in school. Or maybe it even represents just getting dinner on the table after your mom has had a hard day at work. Let's see how your family members are doing.**

Have kids place their marbles just over the starting line. Pause for a few moments.

Say: **Uh-oh. Your family members seem to be stuck, don't they? Maybe they need a little help. Give each person another marble.**

Pretend this marble is you. See if you can come up with a way to help your family member to the finish line.

If kids seem stumped, suggest they shoot their second marbles into the first ones to move them toward the finish line. If you have a large class, let kids blow cotton balls across the finish line, instead of using marbles. After everyone has reached the finish line, have kids sit in a circle with their marbles. Ask:

• **How did your family-member marbles do at first?**

• **What happened after you decided to help?**

• **When are some times the people in your family could use some help in real life? that you could use some help?**

Say: **Everyone needs encouragement at times—even our family members. There's a verse in the Bible that talks about encouraging one another. Let's look at it right now.**

Have a volunteer read aloud Hebrews 10:24 as the rest of the class follows along.

Say: **What a wonderful verse! Just like in our activity, our actions can help our family members, and so can our words and our prayers. Think of one action you can take this week to encourage someone in your family toward love and good deeds. I'll give you a minute to think.**

Pause for a few moments. Then go around the circle and let kids tell the ways they thought of. Let kids take the marbles home to remind them to follow through on their encouraging intentions!

Faces of Kindness

Theme: Kindness

Scripture: Ephesians 4:32

Summary: Kids will make paper-plate mobiles to reflect different faces of kindness.

Preparation: Gather white paper plates, colorful markers, a hole punch, yarn, and clothes hangers.

Gather everyone together. Let each person answer the following questions. If you have a large class, let kids form pairs and tell their partners the answers. Ask:

• **Tell about a time when someone was kind to you. What happened?**

• **Tell about a time when you were kind to someone else. What happened?**

Say: **We know from the Bible that God wants us to be kind to one another. Let me show you the verse I'm thinking of that talks about kindness.**

Have a student read aloud Ephesians 4:32 as others follow along in their Bibles.

Say: **Being kind to someone can take many forms. It can be a simple act of service to another person, like doing your sister's chores for her. It can be reaching out to someone in compassion, like asking the new kid at school to sit with you at lunch. It can be a willingness to forgive someone who's hurt you, all because God has forgiven you. Kindness has many faces. Let's work together to make something to remind us to be kind.**

Explain that kids will be making a "Faces of Kindness" mobile to hang in their meeting area. Show kids the art supplies you set out. Explain that kids can draw hair or a hat on the back of a paper plate. Then on the other side of the plate, instead of drawing a face, they should draw a picture of how they can show kindness.

As kids finish drawing their faces of kindness, punch a hole in the top of each plate, and let kids attach yarn through the hole. The kids can hang the plates at varying levels from a coat hanger. Let kids draw on as many plates as you have time for, making as many mobiles as you have room for. Keep the mobiles hanging in your classroom as reminders of the Bible verse.

Cash Stash

Theme: Generosity

Scripture: Exodus 36:1-7

Summary: Students will work in groups to develop a monthly budget with play money to take a closer look at the priority they place on giving.

Preparation: Photocopy the play money on page 61. You'll need enough so that groups of three or four students can each have around $2,000. Cut apart the cash and place each group's money in a separate envelope. Each group will also need paper and pencils.

Have students form groups of three or four. Give each group an envelope containing $2,000 in play money. Distribute paper and pencils. Students should work together to create a monthly budget that breaks down how they would spend the money. Don't tell them how they should spend their money or on what, but rather let each group make its own decisions. Their money will likely go for things like clothes, food, entertainment, school supplies, hobbies, music, electronics, magazines, and books.

When they've finished, give each group the opportunity to share its budget. Then ask:

- **How much did you set aside to give to God?**
- **How important is this compared to other expenses?**

Ask students to turn to Exodus 36:1-7. Explain that in this passage, the Israelites are following God's instructions for building the tabernacle. Read the verses aloud, then say: **Imagine the pastor making an announcement like this some Sunday at offering time! God had a specific plan in mind. He gave the people the skills and resources they needed to carry out that plan, and he based its success entirely on their willingness to give. He still works that way today!** Ask:

- **What opportunities do you have to give to God?**
- **How does God use what you give to accomplish his will?**
- **How can you be generous if you don't have much money?**
- **How will you be generous this week?**

Close by giving groups the opportunity to rework their budgets, brainstorming ways to use the $2,000 in a more God-pleasing way.

Heavy Burdens

Theme: Dealing With Divorce

Scripture: Philippians 4:6-7; Colossians 3:12-14

Summary: Kids will identify some of the hurts and worries of divorce and learn about giving them to God.

Preparation: You'll need an old pillowcase for each group of four or five students, and heavy items such as bricks, rocks, hymnals, or pew Bibles. Before class, write Philippians 4:6-7 and Colossians 3:12-14 on an overhead transparency. Set up a projector in the classroom.

Have kids form groups of four or five. Give one preteen in each group an old pillowcase. Set a stack of heavy items near each group. Then say: **Today we're going to talk a little bit about divorce. We've all experienced it, either in our own families or in the families of people we know. When a mom and dad split up, it hurts everyone. Put one of the bricks in the bag to represent the hurt of splitting up.**

Now I want you to think of other things about divorce that cause worry or burdens. For example, maybe kids having to spend time in two different homes is a concern. Maybe we're afraid of fights or harsh words, and so on. Go around your circle, and each of you tell one hard thing about divorce. Then someone else in the group should add a brick to the bag while you hold it. Pass the pillowcase on to the next person, and continue naming things and adding items until I tell you to stop.

Allow the activity to continue until the pillowcases are difficult for the kids to hold. Then turn on the overhead projector. Have a student read aloud Philippians 4:6-7. Give kids a chance to share their thoughts about the verses.

Say: **Just a few minutes ago, we were talking about the painful things about divorce. How should we handle these things? This verse tells us not to worry!** Ask:

- **Is it possible not to worry? Why or why not?**
- **Why shouldn't you worry? Why do you worry sometimes?**

Say: **It might seem impossible not to worry, but it's our goal. The reason we don't need to worry is because we can give all our sorrows to God in prayer! When we do that, the Bible tells us that the peace of God will guard and protect our hearts and minds. That's a promise!**

Pass the pillowcase around now, and when it comes to you, take an item out of the bag and put it in the center of your circle to represent giving your fears

and worries to God. When the pillowcases are empty, hold up an empty one and point out how light and easy it is to carry, now that the burdens are gone.

Let's look at another passage to help us handle the hard feelings that come with divorce and other tough situations in our lives. Show the Colossians verse on the overhead, and have a volunteer read it aloud. Talk about how important it is to forgive those who hurt us and to choose love over hate. Drape a pillowcase over yourself, and tell kids that to "put on love" means to make a choice to love instead of hate.

Think of one way you will show God's love in a tough situation this week. Go around your group, and when it's your turn, drape the pillowcase over your shoulders or lap, and tell a way you'll "put on love" this week.

Close by praying: **Lord Jesus, today we give you our fears, concerns, heartaches, wishes, hopes, and dreams. Thank you that we don't have to worry about anything because you promise to take care of us. Help us to trust you this week, to forgive those who hurt us, and to show love to them in all situations. We love you, Lord. Amen.**

TIP

This subject requires extra sensitivity on your part. Try to be familiar with the family situations of the preteens in your class. This will help you guide the discussion as kids open up. During the discussion times, watch the reactions of kids carefully. If a child shares about a special heartache or an abusive home situation, gently offer to talk to the student privately after the class, then steer the conversation to something more positive. Be sure to follow up with the student. All he or she may need is reassurance from you that God is working in his or her situation. Talk to the pastor, if appropriate, and follow any local laws if abusive situations are brought up during the devotion. As with adults, handle everything shared with confidentiality and respect.

Section 4:
Devotions About School

Simple as ABC

Theme: Doing Your Best

Scripture: Romans 12:4-5

Summary: Kids will each play a unique role in singing a song, then will discover that they're each unique in God's creation.

Preparation: None needed.

Assign each student one or more letters of the alphabet, depending on the size of your group. Then have kids line up shoulder to shoulder. Make sure kids stand so their "letters" are *not* in the correct order—the more mixed up, the better!

Say: **We're going to sing a song that you all know, and you will each have a very important part in this production. I want you to do your best!**

Explain that the class will sing the "Alphabet Song," just as they learned it in preschool. As each person's letter(s) comes up, he or she should step forward out of the line and sing the letter's note, then step back. Have the class sing the alphabet several times, each time urging them to sing and step forward faster and faster. After singing, lead kids in a round of applause for themselves, and ask them to sit down.

Say: **What a wonderful job you all did! The alphabet never sounded better!**

Ask: • **What did it take for us to get through the whole alphabet?**

• **What would have happened if one person didn't sing his or her letter?**

Say: **We needed each one of you to do your part in order to sing the whole alphabet. You each had a special role to play, and you did it well! This is kind of like the roles we have in life. Let me explain. Well actually, I'll let the** *Bible* **explain.**

Have a student read aloud Romans 12:4-5 as others follow along in their Bibles. Then ask:

• **How do these verses apply to the activity we just did?**

• **How do these verses apply to your life? change how you live?**

Say: **We all have special gifts that God gave us—things that we're good at and that we can use for God's glory. That's why it's important to do your best with the abilities God gave you. Your gifts come from God—they're not junk. Remember, God has a plan for your life. You may not know what it is yet, but God will lead you step by step. Just do your best along the way and you'll be contributing, just as you did when we sang the song.**

God's Report Card

Theme: Understanding Grades

Scripture: Colossians 3:23

Summary: Students will take a silly quiz and then give themselves "grades."

Preparation: You'll need pencils and a copy of the "Silly Quiz" hand-out (p. 67) for each student.

Say: **Today we're going to be talking about grades. To begin, I'd like to give you a quick pop quiz. All you'll need for this one is your ten fingers. I'm going to ask you a few questions, and I want you to give me your answers by holding up the correct number of fingers. Ready?** Ask:

• **On a scale from one to ten, with one being the lowest, how important do you think grades are?**

• **On a scale from one to ten, with one being the easiest, how easy or difficult is it to get good grades?**

• **On a scale from one to ten, how much do you think grades show who you are as a person?**

Say: **All right! Good job! You all passed! now let's try another quiz.** Give each person the "Silly Quiz" handout and a pencil.

Do your best; this one's important. Give students time to take the quiz. When they're finished, have them self-grade the quizzes and then assign themselves a grade according to the following scale:

1-4 correct: a rectangle

5-7 correct: a triangle

8-10 correct: a wavy line

After students have marked the grades on their papers, ask:

• **How did you feel about this quiz?**

• **Do you think you did well or not so well? Why?**

• **What does the mark at the top of your paper say about who you are?**

Say: **It's always important to work hard in school and at anything you do. But as you can see, the marks at the top of your papers are just marks. They don't have anything to do with the person you are. Let's read a Bible verse to give us further insight.** Have a volunteer read aloud Colossians 3:23. Ask:

• **What does this verse tell you about how you should view your schoolwork? do your schoolwork?**

Say: **Our work in school and anywhere else may not always seem like it makes much sense. We may wonder why we're doing some things, and we may wonder if those things really even matter. The grades we get might seem like they're really important, and if we don't get good grades, we might feel like we're not good enough people. But according to the Bible, if we do everything as if we're doing it for the Lord, we'll be fine. God doesn't give grades.**

Silly Quiz

1. My middle name is _____.

2. The capital of Brazil is _____.

3. The letter after C in the alphabet is _____.

4. The number of miles from the earth to the sun is _____.

5. The holiday we celebrate on December 25 is called_____.

6. The approximate value of pi is_____.

7. The seven colors in the rainbow are _____.

8. The month following February is _____.

9. The number following 99 is _____.

10. The first book of the Bible is _____.

Beating Cheating

Theme: Cheating

Scripture: Matthew 16:26

Summary: Kids will try to get candy from an unreachable piñata, then learn that cheating never pays, no matter how good the end result may appear.

Preparation: Fill a large balloon with small pieces of wrapped candy. Then blow up the balloon and tie it off. Hang it from the ceiling in such a way that no one in your class will be able to jump and reach it.

Allergy Alert

Be aware that some children have food allergies that can be dangerous. Know your children, and consult with parents about allergies their children may have. Also be sure to carefully read food labels, as hidden ingredients can cause allergy-related problems.

Gather kids around your mini-piñata.

Say: **I've filled this little piñata with all kinds of yummy candy. I bet you'd all like some, right? And you can have some. But there's a slight catch. I don't have a stick to hit the piñata, so you'll have to jump up and grab it with your hands. Each of you will get a turn.**

Let each person try to grab the piñata and fail. Then have kids sit down. Ask:

• **Jumping didn't work; what other ways could you get that yummy candy?**

• **What kinds of things do people sometimes really want in real life?**

Say: **Like this candy, sometimes there are things in life that look so enticing that we're ready to do almost anything to get them. Even if it means doing something wrong.**

Take cheating, for example. Sometimes we want that good grade so badly that we might be willing to cheat on a test or an assignment to get it. And then what? We might get the A. We might fool the teacher. We might even fool our friends. But we can't fool God. Listen to what the Bible says about getting something the wrong way.

Have a volunteer read aloud Matthew 16:26 as others follow along. Ask:

• **What does this verse mean?**

• **How could this verse apply to cheating?**

Say: **It doesn't matter what we gain if we've gotten it the wrong way. We can't fool God. Thankfully, we can ask God to forgive us if we've fallen into this trap. Let's take a moment right now to talk to God and ask his forgiveness for the wrong things we've done.** Pause to let kids pray.

If a person were to steal the candy from this piñata and eat it all, he or

she might get really sick. It's the same way with sin. Sin makes our soul sick. But there's always a better way—God's way! Take down the piñata, and let kids enjoy the treats inside.

Pleasing God

Theme: Respecting Authority
Scripture: Hebrews 13:17
Summary: Preteens will role-play school situations that require their obedience and learn that our submission to authority pleases God.
Preparation: None needed.

Ask a volunteer to read aloud Hebrews 13:17 while others follow along in their Bibles. Then have kids answer the following questions with a partner. After each question, have a few kids share their answers with the class.

- **What does this verse tell us to do?**
- **When are we supposed to do it?**
- **Why are we supposed to obey our authorities?**
- **Who are your authorities at school? How well do you obey them?**

Brainstorm briefly with the kids about situations in which they face authorities at school. Then have kids form pairs or trios. Give them a few minutes to practice role-playing a situation at school that involves an authority figure. Tell them to role-play it two ways: not submitting, then submitting to the authority. After a few minutes, have all the groups act out their situations that show them not obeying. Ask:

- **What are the consequences of not obeying authorities at school in situations like these?**

Give kids time to respond, then have them act out their situations again, this time demonstrating obedience. Ask:

- **How does it feel when you obey? Explain.**

Say: **The last part of Hebrews 13:17 says, "Obey them so that their work will be a joy, not a burden, for that would be of no advantage to you."** Ask:

- **What does that mean?**
- **How can obedience be an advantage to you?**
- **How do you think the authorities in your life feel when you obey them?**
- **Are there ever times when it's best to *not* submit to an authority? When?**

Say: **When we submit and obey God-given authority, everyone wins! You can feel good about yourself because you chose to do the right thing, no matter how you feel about it. Your leaders and teachers enjoy being around you** and are happier to help you when you respect their leadership. And most of all, when we submit to our leaders, it makes God happy! He will honor you and bless you when you obey with a cheerful heart, because you're choosing to be like Jesus.

Running the Race

Theme: Competition

Scripture: 1 Corinthians 9:24-25

Summary: Students will build a paper-bag athlete, help him run a race, and talk about the ultimate prize in life.

Preparation: Gather at least six paper grocery bags, two paper lunch bags, newsprint, newspapers, markers, scissors, and packing tape.

Ask:

- **How many of you have ever been in a race?**
- **What does it feel like when you win a race? when you lose?**
- **How would you prepare for a race if you really wanted to win?**

Say: **Let's be trainers and prepare our own Olympic athlete for a race.**

Explain that kids will be making a paper-bag athlete. For the torso, show kids how to stuff a paper grocery bag with crumpled newspapers, then fit an empty bag over the stuffed bag from the open end. For the head, do the same with a paper lunch bag. For arms and legs, twist paper grocery bags into lengths, and tape them to the torso.

Let kids name the athlete and draw a face, hair, and clothes on it. (For extra fun, dress the paper-bag person in real workout clothes.) Then let kids come up with a training regimen for their athlete. Kids can either write their ideas on a sheet of newsprint taped to the wall, or they can actually move the paper arms and legs as if the athlete is practicing.

After kids have developed the training schedule for the athlete, it's time for the race! Have kids line up in single file, with the first person holding the athlete. At your signal, have the person holding the athlete run around the room, then pass the figure to the next person. Continue until everyone has had a turn. Time the entire event. Then let everyone—including the athlete—sit down for a rest!

Say: **Whew! You all must be tired. Let's see how well our athlete ran the race.** Consult your watch. **Our athlete ran the race in exactly** [say the time you recorded]. **That's too bad! The winning time for this race was actually** [name a time faster than what you recorded]. **How disappointing for our athlete,** especially after all that practice! All that hard work for nothing! Ask:

• **Have you ever been like our athlete, where you worked really hard for something but didn't get it? Tell us about it.** Invite several volunteers to share their stories.

Say: **There's nothing wrong with working hard toward a goal. We just need to choose the right goal. This Bible passage will explain what I mean.**

Have a student read aloud 1 Corinthians 9:24-25 as others follow along. Ask:

• **What do you think this verse means? Why?**

• **What prizes in life are you running to win?**

Say: **We only have one shot at this life. So we need to strive for the right prize. As Christians, the prize is one that lasts forever—eternal life with Jesus. But we don't really have to compete for that prize. All we have to do is believe in Jesus, and the prize is ours. Pretty amazing, isn't it?**

There's nothing wrong with working hard to meet goals. But we do need to keep the ultimate goal of eternal life with Jesus as our number one focus. Think about it. What if our athlete here keeled over after the race? It wouldn't matter how fast he had run or how many races he had competed in. If his time on earth were over, all that would matter is whether he believed in Jesus or not. So work hard with the gifts God has given you, but always keep the perfect prize as your focus.

Night School Can Be Cool

Theme: Homework

Scripture: Ecclesiastes 11:6

Summary: Kids will compare and plant seeds and learn that homework is a tool used to "grow" knowledge.

Preparation: Seven to ten days in advance, wrap marigold seeds in damp paper towels, and keep them in several sealed sandwich bags to sprout. Be sure to keep the paper towels moist. Label each bag with the date and time you "planted" the seeds, planting each set of seeds on a different day. You'll also need plastic foam cups, soil, new seeds, rulers, craft sticks, and fine-tipped markers for the devotion.

If marigolds are out of season, you may substitute grass seed, untreated birdseed, or small flower bulbs.

When kids have arrived, ask:

• **Why do you get homework?**

Ask for a volunteer to read aloud Ecclesiastes 11:6 while others follow along in their Bibles. Then ask:

- **Why does this verse tell us to work both day and night?**
- **How might our Bible verse relate to you doing homework?**

Divide the students into small groups, and give each group a sandwich bag to open and a ruler to measure the sprouts. Say: **Today we're going to open some bags that contain seeds which were planted a few days ago. I want you to carefully measure the height of the tallest sprouts and to count how many seeds sprouted in your bag.**

Allow the students a few minutes to do this activity. Ask each group to report to the whole class the time and date its seeds were planted, how many sprouted, and the height of the tallest plants. Then ask:

- **Which seeds grew best?**
- **Did you expect this result? Why or why not?**

Say: **Homework is a little like planting seeds. Even if we don't like homework, it is a necessary part of school. The teacher, like a farmer, doesn't know which assignment at school or at home will help you to learn the topic being taught. We all learn in different ways, at different times. Homework is like night school, giving you another chance to learn what you need to know. To help us remember this, let's each plant a sprouted seed and some new seeds in the cup of soil I give you. You may label the craft sticks with the time and date each seed was planted, to see which ones grow the best in the end.**

Take the cups home to care for them. Bring them back in a week to measure, then send the cups home with children.

I'm So Worried!

Theme: Anxiety

Scripture: Matthew 6:25-34

Summary: Students will rate various situations and events by how anxious the events make them feel. Then they'll discover Scripture's antidote to worrying.

Preparation: You'll need index cards, pencils, paper, markers, newsprint, and masking tape.

On three pieces of paper, write the following: "Really worried," "Kind of worried," and "Not worried at all." Tape the papers to the floor in a line at one end of the room, about three feet apart.

Ask:

• **What are some things in your life that make you feel anxious or worried?**

Give each person two index cards and a pencil.

Say: **On each of your index cards, write one situation or event that makes you feel anxious or worried. Don't write your name. If you can't think of something specific from your own life, write something that you think might make someone else feel anxious or worried. For example, you might write, "Standing up in front of other people to give a speech," or "Hearing my parents fight." I will be reading these aloud, but I won't tell who wrote them.** Give students time to think and write, and then collect the cards.

Point out the signs that you've taped to the floor, and say: **Now I'm going to read these cards aloud. After I read each one, I'd like you to line up behind the paper that best expresses your feelings about the situation. For example, if I read, "Standing up in front of other people to give a speech," and that situation makes you feel really worried, stand behind that sheet of paper.**

Read the situations one at a time, and give students time to line up behind the signs for each one. If you come across a situation that you feel could be embarrassing for a student, skip that card and move on to the next one.

After reading all the cards, ask:

• **What did you notice about yourself and others as you were doing this activity?**

Say: **Now that we've identified some of the things that worry you, let's talk about what you *do* when you feel worried.** Ask:

• **What do you do when you find yourself in any of these situations and you're feeling worried?**

• **Does this help you to feel less worried? Explain.**

Say: **Let's read a Bible passage that will help us to know what we can do when we feel worried.** Have a volunteer read aloud Matthew 6:25-34 while others follow along in their Bibles. Then ask:

• **What does this passage tell us about worry?**

• **What are some things in this passage we could apply to situations we felt worried about?**

On a sheet of newsprint, write the following questions. (You may want to guide students to find these questions from the passage themselves.)

• Is this situation or event more important than my life?

• Can I add a single hour to my life by worrying about this?

• Can God take care of this situation better than I can?

• What can I do instead of worrying about this situation?

Say: **According to this passage, these are some questions we can ask ourselves whenever we feel worried about any situation or event. Let's give it a try.** Randomly distribute the worry cards students wrote earlier. One at a time, have students read aloud the situations, and then lead them to answer the questions for each one.

Close in prayer, asking God to help students to always seek him and his righteousness, especially when they're feeling worried.

Go for the Goal!

Theme: Goals

Scripture: Matthew 25:14-29

Summary: Students will be challenged to set a series of goals in order to complete a simple obstacle course.

Preparation: You'll need to set up a simple obstacle course. The obstacles can be unique to your room and available materials, but some ideas include: crawling under a low table, moving blindfolded through a small maze of chairs, and balancing across a length of wood or a piece of yarn. Try to create at least four unique obstacles for students to encounter. You'll also need index cards and pencils.

Begin by asking:

• **Have you ever set goals for yourself? What were some of those goals?**

• **Did you achieve the goals you set for yourself? What happened?**

Say: **Let's read a Bible passage about some people who set different goals.** Have a volunteer read aloud Matthew 25:14-29. Ask:

• **Think of the man who was given five talents. What do you think his goal might have been? Do you think he achieved his goal?**

• **Think of the man who was given two talents. What do you think his goal might have been? Do you think he achieved his goal?**

• **Now think of the man who was given just one talent. What do you think his goal might have been? Do you think he achieved his goal?**

• **Which man's goal do you think was most pleasing to the master and to God? Why?**

Say: **The men in this story were each given a gift and the responsibility to set goals and use those gifts wisely. The first man set a high goal for himself and his gift, and he worked hard to achieve it. On the other hand, the third man didn't set any goals for himself or his gift, and he didn't achieve anything. In the same way, God gives each of us gifts, and he wants us to set** goals and use our gifts responsibly to achieve great things for him. Let's try some goal-setting now.

Show students the obstacle course, pointing out all of the obstacles they'll need to get through. Ask:

• **What is your overall goal?**

Say: **Your goal is to reach the other side of the room. However, often when we set goals in life, we realize that our goals are too big and we need to set some smaller goals to help us achieve the big goals. Because there are several obstacles in your path across the room, you'll need to set a few smaller goals for yourselves.**

Have students form pairs, and have partners work together to create a series of goals to get themselves across the room. Give each pair an index card and a pencil, and have them write their goals on the card. Walk them through creating their first goal, which will be the specifics of getting through the first obstacle successfully. When each pair has created a set of goals, have them use their goal lists to get them through the obstacle course. When all pairs have finished, ask:

• **Which do you think would have been easier: planning a set of smaller goals to reach your big goal, or just plowing through and trying to reach the big goal without thinking it through first? Explain.**

Say: **Let's think back to the men in the Bible story again. The men all had the same basic goal: to keep the master's money safe. But the first man thought the goal through and realized that if he set a few smaller goals along the way, he might be able to actually give the master more money than he started with. The third man didn't think the goal through, and he just decided to bury the money and not do anything else with it. It was the man with the plan that pleased the master most.**

Give each student an index card and a pencil. Say: **Now I'd like you to think of a goal you have in your life. Think of something big, like getting good grades or making the hockey team. Write your goal on one side of your index card. Next, I want you to think of some smaller goals you might need to set and reach before you attain the big goal. For example, if you have a big goal of getting good grades, some of your smaller goals might include setting up a regular study time, finding a place to write your assignments down, and talking to your parents regularly about how you're doing in school. Write at least three smaller goals on the back of your card.**

If students seem stumped, you might want to have them help each other and brainstorm smaller goals as a group. Encourage students to take their goal cards home with them and put them some place where they'll see them every day. During coming weeks, ask students how they're doing with their smaller goals and their big goals.

Pretty in Punk

Theme: Embarrassment

Scripture: John 5:1-9

Summary: Students will give volunteers a new, punk look and discuss how it feels to look or be different from everyone else.

Preparation: You'll need lots of outlandish, inexpensive make-up samples, styling products, and discarded clothing. Think 1980s—Boy George and Cyndi Lauper. Set all these supplies on a table. Have paper towels and soapy water handy for cleanup afterward.

Check out your local thrift store to find many of these supplies.

Have students form groups of five or six. One person in each group should be a fun-loving, outgoing sort who won't mind lots of attention. This volunteer should act as a model for his or her group.

Direct your students to the table of supplies, which they should share, and encourage each group to go to work transforming their model into a punk rocker! When finished, each group should introduce its creation to the class.

Ask the models:

• **What would it be like to go out in public this way?**

Ask the rest of the kids:

• **Describe a time you felt or looked different.**

Ask students to turn to John 5:1-9. Have some volunteers read the passage aloud. Then say: **This man was in a place where lots of disabled people waited for healing. He'd waited thirty-eight years and had no family or friends to help him into the water when it stirred.**

When this man saw healthy people pass by, perhaps he felt embarrassed. He certainly must have felt awkward when people strolling by looked his way. Ask:

• **How did Jesus respond to this man?**

• **What things make you feel awkward or different?**

• **How does Jesus feel about you, in spite of your weaknesses?**

Close with a time of sharing, giving students the opportunity to tell about embarrassing moments and bolster one another's confidence through words of encouragement.

The Boring Gift

Theme: Boredom

Scripture: Ephesians 4:22-23

Summary: Kids will explore the idea of boredom as a gift to help us change ourselves.

Preparation: You'll need markers, scissors, glue, several magazines, and four pieces of poster board.

Ask:

• **When do you get bored?**

• **What do you do when you're bored?**

Ask a volunteer to read aloud Ephesians 4:22-23 while others follow along in their Bibles.

Say: **I'd like you to think of boredom as a gift. When you're bored, you may be tired of something, find something too easy or too hard, or just need a change. Boredom can be your mind's growing pain, telling you that you need to do something creative with your mind. We're going to try to follow our Bible verse today. I want you to "put off your old self" and have "a new attitude of mind" as you think of new things to do when you are bored.**

Divide students into four groups to brainstorm ways to "grow" their minds when bored at school. Give each group one of the following topics:

Broaden: Combat boredom by doing something creative like writing or cartooning.

Organize: Alleviate boredom by using the time to study or do homework.

Research: Fight boredom with your senses by reading or observing your surroundings.

Exercise: Fight boredom by stretching, or making up routines of tightening and relaxing muscles.

Give each group poster board, magazines, scissors, glue, and markers to make a collage of their topic. After each group has finished, allow them to share their ideas with the whole group.

Recite the four topic words a few times together as a means to remember the different ways to overcome boredom. Point out that the first letter of each word spells B-O-R-E and that God gives us an opportunity to grow and change when we become bored. Ask:

• **How will you fight boredom this week?**

Close by praying together for wisdom and courage to fight boredom whenever we face it.

Section 5:
Devotions About My World

www.God.com

Theme: Internet Wisdom

Scripture: 2 Corinthians 10:5

Summary: Students will analyze fictitious Web site content according to scriptural principles.

Preparation: You'll need a ball of yarn, thumbtacks or masking tape, construction paper, and markers. Using the "www.God.com" handout (p. 80), create a "Web page" on a piece of construction paper for each of the pages described on the handout. These can be as simple or as elaborate as you want—you may choose to create your own simple graphics, or you may choose to just write the text on the construction paper. You'll also need to create a simple "web" in your room by tacking or taping yarn around and across the room. Hang the construction-paper Web pages you've created at various spots along the web.

Ask:

• **How many of you have ever used the Internet?**

• **How do you know what is good and what's not so good on the Internet?**

Say: **The Internet is an amazing tool, and it can be used for many incredible things. However, the Internet is also home to many bad things. Sometimes it's hard to know what's OK— and what's not— when we're using the Internet. Let's look at a Bible verse that might help us to know what's OK to look at and**

use on the Internet. Have a volunteer read aloud 2 Corinthians 10:5 while others follow along in their Bibles. Ask:

• **What do you think it means to "take captive every thought to make it obedient to Christ"?**

• **How might we apply this information to our usage of the Internet?**

Say: **This verse can lead us to ask a couple of questions any time we're unsure about something we're viewing on the Internet. First, we can ask ourselves, "Does this set itself up against the knowledge of God?" In other words, does looking at the information on this Web site bring me closer to Jesus? Or does it go against God's teachings?**

The other question we can ask ourselves is, "Does this inspire thoughts that are obedient to Christ?" Or does it lead my mind where it probably shouldn't go?

Let's use these questions to help us decide what to do about a few pretend Web sites. I've created a "web" of yarn here in our room; you'll see that there are several pages created to look like Web pages. One at a time, I'd like you to travel along the web, just as you would if you were using the Internet. When you come across a Web page, read the information aloud, and we'll all help you ask and answer these questions to decide if it's a Web site you should be looking at.

Have students travel the web, one at a time. Once a person encounters a "Web page," help the group determine what kinds of things might be on that site and answer the questions about the content. If they determine the Web site to be a "keeper," post it on a wall. If it's a "loser," throw the sheet away. Then let another person begin where the first person left off.

After you've gone through the four Web pages, have students form pairs, and give each pair a sheet of construction paper and markers. Have each pair create its own Web site, either one that already exists or their own unique creation. Then have pairs hang their Web pages on the "web," and continue the process.

Once all the Web pages have been examined, ask:

• **How will you better use the Internet on your own?**

Say: **One of the best ways to find out if something is OK for us or not is to talk directly to God about it. Let's do that now. God, we thank you for your gifts of intelligence and technology for us to use. We pray that you will give us your wisdom as we use these great gifts. In Jesus' name, amen.**

If you have access to a computer, you might actually take the students on the Internet to view some Web sites (with discretion, of course!).

www.God.com

Web page 1

International Encyclopedia of World Events
Search this site for anything that's ever happened, anywhere in the world!

Web page 2

The Ultimate Shopping Site
Is your hard-earned money burning a hole in your pocket? Bring it here...we'll help you figure out what to do with it!

Web page 3

Lash, Slash, and Dice
Are you looking for the most violent video games in the world? Well, look no further!

Web page 4

Volunteers Are Us
We're looking for a few good men (and women, too!) to volunteer their time and talents to people who really need them. Could this be you?

Excellent or Praiseworthy?

Theme: Media Choices

Scripture: Philippians 4:8

Summary: Preteens will evaluate their media choices using biblical standards.

Preparation: Before leading this devotion, invite students to bring in a variety of their favorite media: movies, CDs, magazines, video games, books, comic books, Web sites, and so on. Just in case, you should also bring in a large selection of media that preteens would be interested in. You will also need copies of the "Think on These Things" handout (p. 82), one per person, plus some extras.

Begin class by passing around the media that kids have brought in. Let them show off their favorites and check out what other people brought.

After a few minutes, invite kids to turn in their Bibles to Philippians 4:8. Read the verse aloud while kids follow along. Distribute copies of the handout, and let kids read through it. Be prepared to answer any questions kids have about any of the words.

Say: **It's hard to know who to listen to when it comes to choosing our media. These are the criteria that the Bible gives us. Let's see what we can find here that measures up reasonably well.**

Challenge the kids to find some examples in what they've brought that measure up reasonably well to the Bible's standards. Give them several minutes to make their evaluations and choices.

After plenty of time, when kids have found at least a few good examples of media, have them show off what they've found and explain why they chose what they did. Ask:

> **One really good way** to alienate yourself forever from your preteens is to judge them by their media choices. Resist the urge! This devotion equips preteens with the tools they need to evaluate their *own* media choices according to biblical standards—let them practice using those tools in a nonjudgmental atmosphere.

- **How easy or difficult was it to find good examples?**
- **What was the easiest criterion to fulfill? the most difficult? Why?**
- **How will you use this verse to guide you when making choices about media?**

Encourage kids to take their handouts home with them, and make extra copies available as well.

Think on These Things

"Finally, brothers, whatever is true, whatever is noble, whatever is right, whatever is pure, whatever is lovely, whatever is admirable—if anything is excellent or praiseworthy—think about such things" (Philippians 4:8).

But what do those words really mean? Ask yourself the following questions, and you'll get a pretty good idea.

True: Does this tell the truth about God? about Jesus? about people? life? relationships? Or does it tell lies?

Noble: Does this show superior character and morals? Or does it try to drag me down?

Right: Does this feel right? Or would I be embarrassed to have my grandparents or my pastor see me enjoying this?

Pure: Does this nourish and enrich my life, or does it pollute me?

Lovely: Does this express beauty or ugliness?

Admirable: Does this portray actions and attitudes that I should follow? or avoid?

Excellent: Is this well-done artistically, or is it shoddy work? first-class, standout material, or just barely average?

Praiseworthy: Does this have value? Could it win a legitimate award?

Good Recommendations

Theme: Living Out Your Faith

Scripture: 2 Corinthians 3:1-3

Summary: Students will create a prototype "Person of Faith" and then write letters of recommendation for each other as people who live out their faith.

Preparation: You'll need butcher paper, markers, masking tape, sticky notes, paper, and pencils.

Ask:

• **What does it mean to live out your faith?**

• **What does a person who lives out his or her faith look like?**

Ask a volunteer to lie down a length of butcher paper, and trace around him or her. Label the drawing, "A Person of Faith." Hang it on a wall, and give each person some sticky notes and a pencil. Have students brainstorm characteristics of a person who lives out his or her faith. Have them write the characteristics on sticky notes and stick them to the drawing. Encourage students to think of things that go along with parts of the body and stick the notes to those body parts; for example, "Eyes that always look for God's will," or "Ears that hear the cries of people in need."

Once you've created your Person of Faith together, give students each a piece of scratch paper, and ask them to brainstorm on their own how *they* are people of faith. Encourage them to think of specific things they've said or done that show how they are living out their faith in their everyday lives. Once students have come up with their lists, have them form pairs. Encourage partners to share their lists with each other, and ask them to help their partners come up with anything they may not have listed about themselves. Ask students to take this activity seriously and prayerfully.

After each student has a complete list, say: **Now let's see what the Bible has to say about living out our faith.** Have a volunteer read aloud 2 Corinthians 3:1-3 while others follow along in their Bibles. **Paul wrote that when we live out our faith, we act as letters of recommendation for Jesus.** Ask:

• **What is a letter of recommendation? Why would someone write one?**

Say: **A letter of recommendation is something a person asks someone who knows him well to write when he or she is applying for a job or a college. A letter of recommendation tells all of the good things about the person, so that the person reading the letter will want to hire him or her. In the same way, we serve as letters of recommendation for Jesus. When other people** "read" us, or watch our lives and the way we act, they decide whether or not they want to follow Jesus.

Give each person a clean sheet of paper.

Say: **I'd like each of you to write a letter of recommendation for your partner, telling why he or she is a good person of faith. Think of all of the ways your partner is living his or her faith. Address your letter "To anyone watching [person's name]'s life," and then tell that person all of the reasons that you think he or she would want to follow Jesus based on what he or she sees in your partner's life.**

Circulate among students as they're writing to answer questions or provide guidance. When students are finished, have them share their letters with each other.

God's Green Earth

Theme: Caring for Creation

Scripture: Genesis 1:26-31; Psalm 24:1-2

Summary: Preteens will create personal works of art and experience the destruction of their work. Then they'll talk about how to care for God's creation.

Preparation: You'll need plenty of art supplies. Bring more than enough newsprint or art paper for each student, plus watercolor paints and brushes, ink, markers, glitter glue, and whatever other supplies you can get your hands on. Don't forget over-shirts, paper towels, and newspapers or garbage bags to protect surfaces.

Begin by asking preteens to each choose a workplace and supplies to create a very personal work of art. They may create anything they like, but encourage them to especially consider natural subjects, such as land- or seascapes, people, flowers, and animals.

Let the students get well underway on their art projects, and then ask them to stop working. Have them pass their works of art around for others to see or move around to look at others' work. On your signal, preteens should damage the work of art that they are looking at by tearing it, crumpling it, or smudging paint or ink across it. Then have everyone return the artworks to their creators or return to their own works of art.

You know your students best. It's possible that it might not be appropriate for them to destroy each other's work. If that's the case, you do the damage yourself. This might be easier for some kids to accept.

When everyone is rejoined with his or her work of art, ask:

• **How did it feel to create this special, personal piece of art?**

• **How did it feel to see it get trashed?**

• **How did it feel to trash someone else's artwork?**

Ask students to turn to Psalm 24 in their Bibles. Read aloud verses 1-2 while kids follow along. Ask:

• **How is what we just did like what has happened to God's creation?**

Now ask kids to turn to Genesis 1. Ask a volunteer to read aloud verses 26-31. Ask:

• **What job did God give people in the garden?**

• **How do you think God must feel to see the "caretakers" of his world trash his beautiful creation, his masterpiece?**

• **How can you help to restore God's masterpiece? How will you try?**

In closing, have preteens work together to create new works of art that show how they can care for God's creation.

Drawn to God

Theme: Helping the Hopeless

Scripture: Psalm 34:18

Summary: Kids will use a simple science experiment to demonstrate God's healing love.

Preparation: For every three students, you'll need a small paper plate, a magnet, and enough iron shavings or metal paper clips to move around the plate.

Ask:

• **What do you do when you're feeling happy and content?**

• **What makes you feel that way?**

• **What do you do when you're feeling down and hopeless?**

• **What makes you feel that way?**

Say: **Everybody has ups and downs in life. But sometimes people get so down that they feel hopeless and helpless. There's no such thing as being so low that God can't help you. Listen to what the Bible says.**

Have a student read aloud Psalm 34:18 while the rest of the class follows along.

Say: **God is right there when we're feeling hopeless. He's ready to pull us back together again. I'll show you what I mean.**

Have kids form trios, and give each group a paper plate, a magnet, and some iron shavings or paper clips. Have kids group the iron shavings or paper clips together in the center of their plates. Ask kids to slowly call out circumstances that cause people to feel hopeless. Kids might say things like when someone is sick, when someone's parents get divorced, or when a loved one dies.

For each situation kids mention, instruct them to gently move their shavings or paper clips apart. Keep mentioning things until the shavings or paper clips are spread all over the plate.

Say: **See how the shavings** [paper clips] **are spread all over your plate? That's what it's like when someone's life falls apart. It feels as though everything's in pieces and nothing can bring things back together again. But that's not the truth. God is right there, ready to help.** Have kids take turns holding the magnet under the paper plate and moving the shavings or paper clips back together again, as you read each of the following statements about God.

God brings comfort. Pause. **God brings healing.** Pause. **God brings love.** Pause. **God brings other people into your life to help.** Pause. **God brings truth and understanding.**

Just as the magnet brought these shavings [paper clips] **back together, God can heal a broken and hopeless heart. The next time you feel down, be still and trust God to help you. And if you see someone else who's feeling hopeless, encourage them with the good news of God's love.**

Who Are Your True Friends?

Theme: Substance Abuse

Scripture: 1 Corinthians 6:19-20

Summary: Students will hear an allegorical story and then make a commitment to stay drug- and alcohol-free.

Preparation: You'll need copies of the "Commitment" handout (p. 89) and pencils.

Begin by telling this story. Say: **Nick was really proud of his room. When his older brother went to college, his parents let him move into the attic. It was a huge space, with all sorts of cool nooks and crannies. Nick's brother had left some of his furniture up there, including a great couch and a pretty nice stereo. Nick's parents let him redecorate the place, including new paint and carpet. Nick painted the walls in this cool tie-dye pattern, and the carpet was this really soft, plush stuff...awesome! Nick felt almost like he was living in his own apartment or something—he even** had his own bathroom up there!

The first few weeks he lived there, Nick really shocked his mom by keeping his room super clean. He'd always been kind of a slob before, but now that he had such a nice room, he really wanted to keep it looking good.

One day Nick was just hanging out in his room, listening to some music, when without a knock or any warning, the door flew open! In walked Joe, an acquaintance of Nick's from school. In one hand, Joe was carrying a greasy bag full of food from some fast-food place, and in the other he was holding a half-eaten burger—one of those that's supposed to get all over your face. The burger was dripping and oozing mayonnaise and ketchup and who knows what else, and Joe's face was covered with the goo as well. Joe spit out with his full mouth, "Hey, man...how's it goin'? Nice place you got here! Want a fry?" Nick was speechless as he watched Joe's ketchup-and-mayonnaise goo drip all over the new carpet. Joe set the greasy bag on Nick's bed, and the grease quickly sank into his new comforter.

Before Nick could even do anything, in bounded George, another friend from school. George was obviously fresh off the basketball court—he had the smell to prove it! Dripping sweat, George began to pace around Nick's room, stepping on things and knocking things down. He stepped on and broke Nick's favorite DVD without even noticing, and he sent Nick's new lamp crashing to the floor. "Nick, man, what a great room you have here! I just got done with b-ball, and man, am I pumped! Whooeee!" Before long, George had damaged many of Nick's prized possessions and filled the room with his nasty odor.

Before Nick could say a word, both friends had left his room without even a goodbye. Nick just stood in the middle of his room, dumbfounded as he surveyed the damage. Ask:

• **How would you feel if you were Nick?**

• **What would you do if this happened to you?**

Say: **Now imagine that Nick's room represents something different—your body. And the friends that came in and messed things up—they represent drugs and alcohol.** Ask:

• **How might the effects that these friends had on Nick's room be like the effects that drugs and alcohol have on your body?**

• **These people claimed to be Nick's "friends"—do you feel that some people consider drugs and alcohol to be their friends? Explain.**

Say: **Let's hear what the Bible has to say about the way we should treat our bodies.** Have a volunteer read aloud 1 Corinthians 6:19-20. Then ask:

• **What does this passage compare your body to?**

Say: **Just as Nick's room was special to him, our bodies are special and sacred to God. He doesn't want us to put anything in them that will mess them up. He wants us to use our bodies—his special, perfect creations—to worship him. He called our bodies "temples"—he wants to live there. He doesn't want his home to be a vile, gross place.**

Today I'd like to challenge each of you to make a commitment to keep your body a clean, sacred temple for God. I'm challenging you to stay drug- and alcohol-free, to keep those substances out of your temple.

Distribute the "Commitment" handouts (p. 89) and encourage students to sign them.

Commitment

I, _____, today make a promise and commitment before God and these witnesses to stay away from the false friends of drugs and alcohol. I commit myself to keeping my body a clean, holy, pure, temple for God to dwell in.

_____
(signature)

_____
(date)

Smoke Alarm

Theme: Smoking

Scripture: 1 Peter 2:11

Summary: Kids will use an experiment to illustrate how smoking can trap us into the prison of addiction.

Preparation: You'll need a peeled, hard-boiled egg for every pair of kids, tissues, markers, a lighter, and jars with openings that snuggly fit an egg.

Try this experiment at home first to make sure it works and that you have chosen the right size jars. Small eggs work best with 20-ounce plastic sports drink bottles with wide tops, while jumbo eggs work best with 10-ounce or smaller tapered glass condiment jars. Be sure that your mouth can fit around the mouth of the jar, in order to remove the eggs whole.

To get the eggs out whole, remove ashes and tilt the jar so that the egg is near the opening but not blocking it. Seal the opening with your mouth, blow hard into the jar, and remove the jar from your mouth quickly, tilting the opening down.

Have preteens turn in their Bibles to 1 Peter 2:11. Have a volunteer read this verse aloud. Then ask:

• **How can something cause us to war against our soul?**

• **Why is smoking bad for you?**

Have kids form pairs. Give each pair a peeled, hard-boiled egg and markers. Ask them to draw a face on the egg so that the smaller end of the egg is the bottom of the face. Give each pair a tissue, and ask them to draw a cigarette or cigar on the tissue. Hand each pair a bottle or jar, and ask them to place the tissue in the bottom.

Say: **Today we're going to use an experiment to see how smoking can trap you into becoming addicted. Put your egg face onto the top of the jar, small end down, and give it a tap to show that it fits snuggly but won't go in. As I come around, I'm going to ask you to lift the egg, let me light the tissue inside the jar, and then place the egg back on top immediately. You must keep your sleeves and hair back as I light the tissue.**

Do not let the students use the candle lighter. You must supervise this step carefully by doing it yourself. Ask:

• **What happened to the eggs?**

Say: **If any eggs have not been sucked into the jars, I want you to tap them again and see them go inside. The smoking tissue caused your egg people to become trapped inside the jars. This experiment shows how easy it is to get sucked into a bad situation, like the invisible prison of addiction.**

Ask the kids to share with their partners ways that addictions cause "war" within us and affect our relationship with God.

Say: **Now I want you to get the eggs out of the jars in one piece.** Give students a few moments to try. Then explain that God can always help us in any situation, but it's best not to get into trouble in the first place. Show them how to remove the eggs.

Here Today, Gone Tomorrow

Theme: Materialism

Scripture: Matthew 6:19-21

Summary: Kids will research history books to find things that don't exist anymore. Then they'll read the Bible's advice about where to keep their focus.

Preparation: You'll need old encyclopedias or history books on specific subjects, such as early flight. Books with pictures would make reference easier. You'll need at least four books, but the more the better. You'll also need paper and pencils.

Have kids form four groups, and give each group at least one of the history books you brought in. Also supply each group with paper and pencils.

Say: **Today I want you to work with your group members to find things in these books that no longer exist. I don't mean *people,* I mean *things* that don't exist anymore. You might find buildings, artwork, ships, inventions, businesses, or even countries. Work together to make a list of as many of these things as you can. You have five minutes. Go!**

After five minutes, call time. Let groups take turns presenting their lists to the rest of the class. Then have kids discuss the following questions in their groups. After each question, invite volunteers to share their answers with the rest of the class. Ask:

• **Why were the things you named important to people at the time they existed? Explain.**

• **How hard do you think people worked to create and maintain the things you named? Give examples.**

Say: **I'm sure some people worked hard to make the things you named. People invested time, hard work, and lots of money in many things that no longer exist. Maybe some people even ignored their families and their morals and God—just to develop and hold on to these things. The Bible has something to say about that.**

Have kids read aloud Matthew 16:19-21 in their groups. Ask:

• **What do these verses tell us about putting our faith and energy into material things?**

• **Where does God want you to invest your heart? How will you do so this week?**

Explain that when we set our sights and hearts on things that won't last, it's an effort in futility. Only God and his love provide everlasting benefits. Have kids pray in their groups, asking God to help them keep their focus on him, rather than material wealth or possessions.

Psychic Savvy

Theme: Avoiding the Occult

Scripture: 1 Kings 18:22-39

Summary: Students will test their clairvoyant abilities by making predictions about their classmates, to open a discussion about the dangers of the occult.

Preparation: You'll need three slips of paper per student, pencils, and a hat or basket.

As students arrive, give them each three slips of paper and a pencil. Ask them to secretly write on the slips three things that no one else in the class would know about them. They should fold their completed slips and place them in a hat or basket.

When everyone has finished, each person should draw three pieces of paper from the hat or basket, read aloud what is written, and try to guess which person each clue applies to.

After everyone has had the chance to guess, reveal the true answers, and rate everyone's "psychic powers." Turn to a more serious tone. Ask:

• **What practices are commonly associated with the occult?**

• **How does God feel about these activities?**

Ask students to read aloud 1 Kings 18:22-39, a few verses each. Then ask students what similarities they see between the prophets of Baal and people today who worship false gods or even Satan.

Say: **Things like psychics, horoscopes, Ouija boards, and witchcraft may seem funny or even like a game. But these activities are the same as blatantly worshipping a false god. We should trust the true God instead of relying on occult practices to decipher our future.** Ask:

• **How did Baal measure up to God?**

• **When people participate in occult practices, who are they really worshipping?**

- **How does God feel about idolatry?**
- **Why is God better equipped than any false god to help you with your future? In what ways do you ask for God's guidance?**

Close by challenging students to go to God alone for guidance.

Happy Birthday!

Theme: Grief and Death

Scripture: Revelation 21:4

Summary: Kids will discuss the difference between birthdays and funerals, read about how perfect heaven will be, and celebrate the new birth of eternal life with God.

Preparation: Gather party supplies such as balloons, crepe paper, tape, birthday cake, paper plates, utensils, napkins, cups, and drinks.

Say: **Let's talk for a few minutes about events that people commemorate. First let's discuss birthdays.** Ask:

- **Why do people celebrate birthdays?**
- **How do people celebrate birthdays?**

Allergy Alert

Be aware that some children have food allergies that can be dangerous. Know your children, and consult with parents about allergies their children may have. Also be sure to carefully read food labels, as hidden ingredients can cause allergy-related problems.

- **What are some words you'd use to describe birthday celebrations?**
- **Now think about funerals; how are they different from birthday celebrations?**
- **What are some words you'd use to describe funerals?**
- **Has anyone here been to a funeral? What was it like?**

Say: **Birthdays are usually happy occasions, with parties, balloons, cakes, and gifts. Funerals are usually somber occasions, with tears, quiet voices, and sadness. But I'd like to propose a change of thought today. If a person is a Christian, his or her funeral should really be a celebration! Maybe this Bible verse will explain what I mean.**

Have a volunteer read aloud Revelation 21:4 as others follow along in their Bibles.

Say: **We celebrate birthdays because birthdays are all about new beginnings. Funerals can be, too. When a Christian dies and goes to heaven, that person will never experience tears or sickness or sadness again. It's a whole**

new start to a wonderful and perfect existence. That's a reason to celebrate!

Show kids the party supplies and snacks you brought. Explain that you're going to have a "birthday party" for all the Christians who have started new lives in heaven. If appropriate, invite kids to name Christians they know who have died, so the party has more personal significance. Let kids decorate and enjoy food and time together as they discuss what they think heaven will be like.

Section 6:
Devotions About Special Days

New *Every* Morning

Theme: New Year's Day

Scripture: Isaiah 40:28-31

Summary: Preteens will listen to a song and talk about the lyrics. Then they will hold books and talk about new strength with God.

Preparation: You'll need the song "New Day" by Joy Williams *(By Surprise)* and a CD player. You'll also need hymn books or pew Bibles, two per preteen.

Play the song "New Day" by Joy Williams. Ask students to listen carefully to the lyrics. You might need to play the song twice. Then ask:

> **Feel free to use a different,** newer song for this devotion if you prefer. Some other songs that would work well include "New Year's Day" by Carolyn Arends *(Feel Free)*, "Call On Jesus" by Nicole C. Mullen *(Talk About It)*, "For the Moments I Feel Faint" by Relient K *(The Anatomy of the Tongue in Cheek)*, and "Resolution" by The O.C. Supertones *(O.C. Supertones Live, Vol. 1)*.

• **Do you ever make New Year's resolutions? Like what?**

• **How long do they usually last?**

• **How do you feel when you stop doing whatever you resolved to do?**

• **How are the lyrics of this song like New Year's Day?**

• **Does God give us only one new chance per year? Explain.**

Now have the kids stand up and stretch out their arms with their palms facing up. Place a Bible or hymnal on each hand. Ask the kids to stand that way for as long as they can. After several kids give up, tell the rest to relax as well. Ask:

- **How did you feel when I first put the books on your hands?**
- **How is that like when you first make a New Year's resolution?**
- **How did you feel after holding the books for a while?**
- **How is that like when you don't keep a New Year's resolution?**

Have preteens turn to Isaiah 40:28-31 in their Bibles. Read the verses aloud while they follow along. Then say: **God gives us new strength, new hope, new chances every day. God doesn't limit our second chances to New Year's Day. With God, every day is a new day.**

You've Got to Stand for Something

Theme: Martin Luther King Jr.

Scripture: Philippians 3:12

Summary: Students will experience standing up for things they believe in.

Preparation: You'll need pencils and copies of the "You've Got to Stand for Something" handout (p. 97), one per student.

Say: **I'm going to read a series of scenarios. When I finish each one, if you feel like you could stand up for yourself or others in that situation, stand up.** Read through the scenarios on the "You've Got to Stand for Something" handout (p. 97) one at a time, and give students time to stand. Have them sit down to hear the next scenario. When you're finished, say: **Standing up in situations like these always requires a risk. You might risk looking stupid in front of friends, or you could even risk your safety or your life.**

The Rev. Martin Luther King Jr. was a man who stood for something—the equality of African Americans. He took a big risk to make his stand, and he ended up losing his life. While we may not be faced with such a drastic consequence, we still take risks when we stand up for God and what we know is right.

Give each person a copy of the "You've Got to Stand for Something" handout and a pencil. Have students each choose one of the scenarios that you read earlier and answer the questions. When they're finished, have students form groups according to the scenarios they chose and share their answers.

Read aloud Philippians 3:12. Ask:

- **How might these words be applied in the situations you discussed?**

Say: **When we take a chance and risk looking stupid, or even getting hurt, in order to stand up for what we know is right, we bring ourselves ever closer to what Jesus wants us to be. We can challenge ourselves and others to continue to press on toward this goal.**

You've Got to Stand for Something

Scenario 1

You're hanging out at your best friend's house. There are several other people there, including some of the really popular kids from school. Everyone is kind of bored. Then one of the popular kids says, "Hey, you wanna have some real fun? There's gotta be some alcohol around here somewhere!" He starts rummaging through the cabinets, searching for alcohol.

Could you stand up to this person?

Scenario 2

You're in science class. The teacher is discussing Creation vs. Evolution. Suddenly, he begins picking on another student. This girl goes to your youth group, but you don't know her well. The teacher begins ridiculing her about being a Christian and believing that the entire earth could have possibly been created in seven days.

Could you stand up to this person?

Scenario 3

You're in the cafeteria when a new student walks in, looking for a place to sit. He's wearing old, ratty clothes, and you've heard a rumor that he's living in a tent with his family because they can't afford a place to live. The people at your table start making rude comments about the student, just loud enough for him to hear. With a frown on his face, the new student turns around and walks out of the cafeteria.

Could you stand up to these people?

Scenario 4

Your team made it to the finals. Toward the end of the game, one of your teammates commits a foul in a crowded situation. The ref calls a penalty on your teammate. Your coach and the other players start arguing with the ref and blaming the foul on the other team. You had a clear view of the play, and you know the ref's call was a fair one—but it could cost you the game.

Could you stand up in this situation?

1. Have you ever been in a situation like this one? Describe your experience. If you haven't been in a situation like this, can you imagine it happening to you? Describe your thoughts.

2. What are some specific things you might do or say in this situation to stand up for what you believe in?

3. What risks might you take if you were to stand up in this situation? For example, would you look dumb or get physically hurt?

4. What might the outcome be if you stood up in this situation?

Loops of Love

Theme: Valentine's Day

Scripture: 1 Corinthians 13:4-8a; 1 John 4:8b

Summary: Kids will discover God's definition of love as well as the fact that God *is* love. Then they'll connect those two concepts and make paper-chain reminders of what they've learned.

Preparation: You'll need scissors, construction paper, fine-tipped markers, and tape.

Say: **It's time to celebrate Valentine's Day, and you know what that means—it's time to talk about love! Now I know that we usually think about romantic love at this time of year, but right now I want to talk about love in general.**

Have kids form pairs to discuss these questions. Invite volunteers to share their answers with the rest of the class after each question. Ask:

• **What is your definition of love? Why do you define it this way?**

• **Where does love come from?**

Say: **The Bible gives us answers to both of those questions. First let's find out where love comes from.**

Have partners read 1 John 4:8b. Say: **The Bible says that God is love. It doesn't just say that God is loving or that God promotes love. It says that God *is* love! That means that all love starts with God and comes from God. God is the author of love. He's the perfect example of love. Now let's see what God's definition of love is.**

Have partners read 1 Corinthians 13:4-8a.

Say: **These verses give us a wonderful picture of love, don't they? And because God is love, he has every one of the characteristics of love that you just read. Let's make something to remind us of our loving God.**

Have kids cut the paper into strips big enough to write on. Each person will need at least fifteen strips. On their paper strips, have kids write each of the characteristics of love from 1 Corinthians 13:4-8a, one per strip. Explain that they should substitute the name "God" for the word *love*. For example, the paper strips should read, "God is patient," "God is kind," and so on.

When they're finished, have kids each make a paper chain by looping the paper strips, writing side out, and taping the ends. Say: **God is love, and his love never ends, just as a circle has no end.** Have kids tape the two ends of their paper chains together to form a circle of love. Encourage kids to take their "loops of love" paper chains home to remind them of God and his love.

Easter Victory

Theme: Easter

Scripture: John 20:10-16; Romans 8:38-39

Summary: Kids will see that Jesus is always part of our lives and that no one can take him away from us.

Preparation: You'll need markers, masking tape, and six pieces of poster board.

Ask a volunteer to read aloud John 20:10-16 while others follow along in their Bibles. Ask:

- **How do you think Mary felt on that first Easter?**
- **Why do you think she didn't recognize Jesus?**

Say: **The first Easter was exciting, but confusing, to Jesus' disciples. These verses tell us that Mary did not recognize Jesus until he said her name. She thought someone had taken Jesus away and didn't realize he was standing right beside her. Jesus wanted Mary to know that no one could ever take him away. He called her name to let her know that he was there with her. The victory of Easter is that we have Jesus always with us, a personal, living Savior who knows us by name.**

Have students form six groups, and assign each group one of the following: our **C**ommunity, **H**ome, **R**ecreation, **I**dentity, **S**chool, and **T**ime. A group can be one person. Explain that each group should brainstorm how they could include Jesus in their lives in the assigned category. They should write their ideas on the poster board.

Have each group share their ideas with the class, and hang each poster so that the first letter of each topic will spell C-H-R-I-S-T. Ask:

- **How do you know Jesus is with you today?**
- **What are you going to do to include Jesus more in your daily life?**
- **Why is Easter important to us?**

Say: **We include Jesus because he loved us enough to die for our sins. Whether we always recognize Jesus in our lives, or whether we always include him, the joy of Easter is that he is always with us. The first letter of each of our topics spells "Christ" to remind us that he is always close to us. We celebrate that nothing can take him away from us, because Jesus is alive and well.**

Read aloud Romans 8:38-39 as a closing prayer.

Mom Mimes

Theme: Mother's Day

Scripture: Proverbs 31:10, 26-31

Summary: Students will act out various activities that a mother might do, while their classmates make guesses about what is being pantomimed.

Preparation: On slips of paper, write different things a mother might do in a day: clean the bathroom, wash dishes, feed the dog, drive the car pool, bake a cake, burp a baby, go to work, balance a checkbook, coach a baseball team, and so on. Fold the strips, and place them in a basket or hat. Have construction paper and markers on hand.

Welcome students and ask them to form two teams. Volunteers from each team should take turns drawing a slip of paper and pantomiming what is written on it, while their teammates try to guess what they are acting out. Afterward, see who can guess the common theme—all the activities are things mothers do to serve others daily. Ask:

• **What do you most appreciate about your mom?**

Be sensitive to students who may not have a mother in their lives by generalizing these questions if needed. Ask a volunteer to read aloud Proverbs 31:10, 26-31. Ask:

• **What qualities would you include in your own, modern-day version of this passage?**

Say: **These verses may seem impossible to live up to, but they give us a good idea of the many sacrifices mothers make for their families. They often put the needs and wants of others ahead of their own.** Ask:

• **What sacrifices do mothers sometimes make?**

• **How can you be more appreciative of all your mom does for you?**

• **How will you show her what she means to you this Mother's Day?**

• **How can you encourage the moms you know?**

Close by giving students the opportunity to create a Mother's Day card for their mom or someone special to them.

Father Says

Theme: Father's Day

Scripture: Proverbs 23:22a

Summary: Kids will learn that God wants them to listen to their fathers. Then they'll make books of fatherly proverbs to give to their dads as proof that they've been listening.

Preparation: Tape a sheet of newsprint to the wall. Set out construction paper, white or light-colored paper, fine-tipped markers or colored pens, and staplers.

Gather kids near the newsprint you taped on the wall.

Say: **It's close to Father's Day, so let's talk about fathers for a few minutes. One thing I know about fathers is that they try to teach their children how to live. They use their experiences and what they've learned in life to try to guide their children. And it's important that we listen to our fathers. In fact, that's exactly what the Bible tells us to do.**

> **TIP**
>
> Be sensitive to kids who don't **have fathers** or whose fathers aren't involved in their lives. Rather than offend those kids, change the wording of this activity to talk about parents or caregivers.

Have a volunteer read aloud Proverbs 23:22a as the other students follow along in their own Bibles.

Say: **Let's see how well you've followed the Bible's advice and listened to your fathers. Let's write some proverbs based on your fathers' advice.**

Have kids take turns calling out advice their fathers have given them. Encourage kids to phrase the advice in single sentences. Write the "proverbs" kids call out on the newsprint. Let kids call out as many proverbs as they can think of.

Say: **Thanks for sharing your fathers' advice. The Bible tells us to listen to our fathers. Let's make something to give to our fathers to show them we've been listening.**

Give kids paper and fine-tipped markers or colored pens. Set out construction paper and staplers. Show kids how to stack several sheets of paper together, then fold them in half. Fold a sheet of construction paper as a cover, and place the folded papers inside. Staple the folded edges together to form a booklet. Tell kids to write one proverb based on their fathers' advice on each page of the booklet. Have kids decorate and personalize the covers, then take them home to give to their fathers.

I Pledge Allegiance...

Theme: Fourth of July

Scripture: Romans 6:15-18

Summary: Students will write their own "declarations of independence" from sin and death.

Preparation: You'll need newsprint, markers, masking tape, paper, and pencils. On the newsprint, write the following:

> • *Preamble:* Write a statement of your intention.

> • *Declaration of rights:* Tell what living as a Christian means to you.

> • *Declaration of complaints:* Tell what it feels like to live in sin.

> • *Declaration of independence:* State that from now on, you will walk with Christ and away from sin.

Use this information to help you create your own model declaration of independence to share with students.

Ask:

• **What do we celebrate on the Fourth of July?**

Say: **The Fourth of July, or Independence Day, celebrates the day when the American colonies finally gained their independence from England and became their own country.** Ask:

• **Why did the colonists want independence from England?**

Say: **The colonists wanted to be free from England so that they could make their own decisions about how they would live their lives. They wanted to be their own country—America—so that they would not have to obey England's king anymore.** Ask:

• **How do you think the colonists' desire for freedom from England might be like your desire for freedom from sin?**

Say: **Just as the colonists wanted freedom from England, we as Christians long to be free from the bondage of sin. We want to be as close to God as possible, not dragged down by the burdens of our sins. Let's hear more about our freedom in Christ.** Ask a volunteer to read aloud Romans 6:15-18. Ask:

• **According to this passage, what are we slaves to? What enslaves you?**

Say: **When we are set free from sin, we become slaves to righteousness, and to God, which is the truest form of freedom.**

Today we're going to write our own personal declarations of independence—declaring ourselves free from sin and death and free to follow God.

Give each student a sheet of paper and a pencil.

Share your own model declaration with them as you go. Then have them give it a try. Circulate among them as they work, offering help and guidance.

When students have finished, post the declarations on the wall where everyone can see them. Remind students to look at them often and to remember their freedom from sin and freedom to live with God.

If you have students who have not yet made faith decisions, guide them through this activity by saying things like, "If you are considering a commitment to Christ, write in your declaration how you think deliverance from sin might feel."

Attitude Check

Theme: Back to School

Scripture: Matthew 13:1-23

Summary: Students will role-play various responses to situations they may face at the beginning of school.

Preparation: You'll need index cards, pencils, and two small containers.

Ask:

• **How do you feel when you're about to go back to school for a new school year? Why?**

• **What are some situations you might face at the beginning of a new school year?**

Have students brainstorm various situations they might face, both good and bad. Some examples are being in a class with no one you know, getting lost in a new school, and feeling excited about new classes.

Give each student an index card and a pencil, and have them each write one possible situation on their index cards. Put those cards in one of the containers.

Next have students brainstorm a list of attitudes or emotions they might feel as they face some of those situations, such as happy, sad, angry, or embarrassed. Write each of the attitudes on an index card, and put those cards in the other container.

Say: **When we head back to school, we'll face many different situations, both good and bad. It's up to *us* how we handle those situations. We can be positive or negative. Let's hear a parable about how our attitudes can affect what happens to us in various situations.** Have a few volunteers read aloud Matthew 13:1-23. Then ask:

• **Which type of soil might represent a good attitude?**

- Which type of soil might represent a not-so-good attitude?
- What happened to the "good attitude" soil?
- What sort of soil are you?

Say: **No matter what situations we're faced with, we always have a choice. We can respond with a positive attitude or a negative attitude—the choice is always ours. Let's experiment with some different attitudes in these situations.**

Have students come up, one at a time, and draw one card from the situation container and one card from the attitude container. Ask the student to create a brief, impromptu role-play to demonstrate the assigned attitude in the given situation. He or she may recruit other actors. After each role-play, ask:

- Have any of you ever dealt with this situation? Explain.
- Did you respond in this way or in a different way?
- Do you think this was the best way to respond? Why or why not?
- What would have been a better way to respond?

Say: **During the first days of school, and in our lives in general, we will face many different situations, both good ones and bad ones. If we can be open to any situation and strive to respond to whatever comes with a positive attitude, our lives will be much better.**

Thanks, God!

Theme: Thanksgiving

Scripture: Psalm 95:1-7a

Summary: Preteens will read a psalm of Thanksgiving, play a game about counting their blessings, and sing songs of thanks.

Preparation: You'll need song books or song sheets, and possibly some kind of accompaniment for kids' singing.

Have preteens sit in a circle, on chairs, or on the floor. Ask them to turn in their Bibles to Psalm 95. Have them take turns each reading one verse aloud, through verse 7a.

Explain that you're going to play a Thanksgiving game. The first person must name one thing he or she is thankful for, saying, "I'm thankful for _____." The next person must say, "I'm thankful for _____," repeating what the first person said, and adding something new. As you go around the circle, each person has to repeat what all the others have said before and then add something new. No repeats allowed! When someone gets stuck, let the others help him or her. Continue until everyone has mentioned one thing that he or she is thankful for. For a different twist on the game, have kids name things they're thankful for in alphabetical order.

After the game, close by singing several of kids' favorite Thanksgiving songs together. Some of these might include "Praise and Thanksgiving," "Now Thank We All Our God," "For Health and Strength," "Thanks Be to God," "Gracias, Señor," "I Will Give Thanks to the Lord," "Give Thanks to the Lord for He Is Good," and "We Praise You, O God."

Lighting the Way

Theme: Christmas

Scripture: Genesis 1:1-4; John 1:1-4

Summary: Kids will discuss the uses and meaning of light and how Jesus is our light.

Preparation: Gather a flashlight for each preteen, plus a candle in a stand, a lighter, and a replica of a manger with baby Jesus, large enough to be seen clearly from a few feet away. Place the candle near the manger on the floor so that the students can sit around these objects at a safe distance. Copy the "Light of the World" handout (p. 108), and cut the paper to separate the readings.

Have kids sit in a circle around the manger and candle. Say: **Christmas was originally a time to celebrate Jesus as the light of the world. Although today we think of Christmas as Jesus' birthday, we also praise God for lighting our way with Jesus, his Son.**

Give each person a portion of the handout to read, in order around the circle. If you have more than eight students, make additional copies and have small groups of students read some portions together.

Dim the classroom lights until Reader 6 says, "Let there be light." Then light the candle beside the manger. Have the kids continue reading. When they're finished, enjoy a moment of silence in the candlelight.

Say: **Light is so important that it was the first gift God gave to the world. I would like you to think of all the ways we use light. Let's take turns each naming one use for light. After you answer, I will give you a light to hold, but you must not turn it on until I tell you to.**

Give each person a chance to speak, and give each one a flashlight after they name a way we use light. Then ask:

• **How do you feel when you see light?**

• **Why do you think Jesus is called the light of the world?**

Say: **John deliberately wrote the beginning of his book to sound like Genesis. He wanted to show that Jesus is God's gift of light to us. Let's share how Jesus, the light of the world, helps us. After you share, please turn on your light and shine it on the baby Jesus. This will remind us that Jesus is our light.**

When all the lights are shining on the manger, close by singing together the first verse of "O Little Town of Bethlehem."

Light of the World

Reader 1: "In the beginning was the Word, and the Word was with God, and the Word was God" (John 1:1).

Reader 2: "In the beginning God created the heavens and the earth" (Genesis 1:1).

Reader 3: "He was with God in the beginning" (John 1:2).

Reader 4: "Now the earth was formless and empty, darkness was over the surface of the deep, and the Spirit of God was hovering over the waters" (Genesis 1:2).

Reader 5: "Through him all things were made; without him nothing was made that has been made" (John 1:3).

Reader 6: "And God said, 'Let there be light,' and there was light" (Genesis 1:3).

Reader 7: "In him was life, and that life was the light of men" (John 1:4).

Reader 8: "God saw that the light was good, and he separated the light from the darkness" (Genesis 1:4).

Scripture Index

Theme Index

Evaluation for

The Ultimate Book of Preteen Devotions

Please help Group Publishing, Inc., continue to provide innovative and useful resources for ministry. Please take a moment to fill out this evaluation and mail or fax it to us. Thanks!

Group Publishing, Inc.
Attention: Product Development
P.O. Box 481
Loveland, CO 80539
Fax: (970) 292-4370

1. As a whole, this book has been (circle one)

not very helpful   *very helpful*

1   2   3   4   5   6   7   8   9   10

2. The best things about this book:

3. Ways this book could be improved:

4. Things I will change because of this book:

5. Other books I'd like to see Group publish in the future:

6. Would you be interested in field-testing future Group products and giving us your feedback? If so, please fill in the information below:

Name _____

Church Name_____

Denomination _____ Church Size _____

Church Address _____

City _____ State _____ ZIP _____

Church Phone _____

E-mail _____